Obeying Jesus

Obeying Jesus...
The 7 commands for every disciple

"Go and make disciples...teaching them to obey all that I have commanded"
  - Matthew 28:19, 20

STEVE DUPLESSIE

ANAPAUO PRESS, ATTLEBORO, MA
2012

Obeying Jesus: The 7 commands for every disciple
Expanded Second Edition with Study Guide

DuPlessie, J. Stephen, 1952-

© 2011, 2012 by Steve DuPlessie. All rights reserved.

Published by Anapauo Press
47 Patterson Street, Attleboro, Massachusetts

First edition – April, 2011
Second expanded edition – August, 2012

ISBN 978-0615657288

Printed in the United States of America

Cover design by Erika Houghton
Author photo by Armando Bettencourt
Front cover photo by iStockphoto.com

Unless otherwise noted, all Scriptures are taken from
THE HOLY BIBLE, NEW INTERNATIONAL VERSION®, NIV® Copyright © 1973, 1978, 1984, 2011
by Biblica, Inc.™ Used by permission. All rights reserved worldwide.

Without limiting the rights under copyright reserved above, no part of this publication may be reproduced, stored in or introduced into a retrieval system, or transmitted, in any form, or by any means (electronic, mechanical, photocopying, recording, scanning or otherwise), without the prior written permission of the copyright owner of this book.

The scanning, duplication and distribution of this book via the Internet or via any other means without permission of the author is illegal and punishable by law. Please purchase only authorized electronic editions, and so not participate in or encourage electronic piracy of copyrighted materials. Your support of the author's rights is appreciated.

The publisher does not have any control over and does not assume any responsibility for third-party Web sites or their contents.

Dedicated with love to Deb,
my bride and life partner of more than 36 years,
and without whose love and support
I would not be who I am today.

Contents

Acknowledgments

Introduction

Chapter 1	Important Last Words	1
Chapter 2	Danger! Danger! Danger!	7
Chapter 3	Command #1: Repent & Believe	14
Chapter 4	Command #2: Be Baptized	24
Chapter 5	"Dead man walking"	31
Chapter 6	Command #3: Remember Me	37
Chapter 7	Command #4: Pray	49
Chapter 8	Command #5: Love God ...	61
Chapter 9	... Love One Another	79
Chapter 10	... And Love Your Neighbor	89
Chapter 11	Command #6: Give	98
Chapter 12	Command #7: Make Disciples	105
Chapter 13	Obeying Jesus	117

Appendix A List of the Commands of Jesus 133

Acknowledgments

The idea behind this project came from an article by George Patterson, formerly a missionary for 21 years in northern Honduras and later of the faculty in the Division of Intercultural Studies at Western Seminary in Portland, Oregon. George's essay, "The Spontaneous Multiplication of Churches," stimulated my thoughts on the challenge of obeying the commands of Jesus—just one more piece of sweet fruit from the *Perspectives on the World Christian Movement* classes, an extraordinarily profitable and challenging course on God's global mission that I took in the spring of 2008.

The thoughts in this book all came together through an opportunity to teach a series in the summer of 2010 on "Obeying Jesus" at Good News Bible Chapel, in Attleboro, Massachusetts where I serve as an elder and the Teaching Pastor. Thanks to my fellow elders and the assembly of Christ-followers at the Chapel for their encouragement, support and conversations around this theme. *High five* to Jeff Cambridge, Ben Harris, Ethan Tirrell and Zach Stebbings for collaborating with me on that summer team-teaching series. I trust that God will use each of you to his glory.

Dennis Fuqua, President of *International Renewal Ministries,* Vancouver, Washington, inspired me to consider turning my thoughts into a book during our discussion of his own insightful book, *Living Prayer: the Lord's Prayer alive in you* (2010). I am grateful for his review of the manuscript and many of Dennis' thoughts are underneath the chapter on Prayer.

I have appreciated the encouragement of Frank Tully, a Navigators staff member currently serving in Australia and once the Director of *The Pierce Fellowship* at The Center for Urban Ministerial Education (CUME) on the inner-city Boston campus of Gordon-Conwell Theological

Seminary. I was privileged to be a Pierce Fellow for four years as a student at GCTS and Frank became a good friend as well as a very helpful mentor. Thanks Frank for offering the Pierce Fellows an acrostic outline on "The discipling practices of Jesus" which I adapted and expanded upon in chapter eleven.

I'm grateful to my life-long friend, son in Christ, and yoke-fellow in ministry, Tom Sharkey, currently the Senior Pastor of First Covenant Church, Youngstown, Ohio, for reading the early manuscript and offering some great observations.

Many thanks to Jon Loveless, my son-in-law, for his careful review of the manuscript, helpful suggestions and careful checking of the Bible references.

I owe a debt to my son Matt for his patient and meticulous critique of the developing manuscript drafts and very gentle corrections of my errors, his keen insights on the content, and his useful editorial suggestions.

Rob Tyler, the Executive Director of *ECS Ministries,* offered detailed editorial recommendations and I am appreciative.

Erika Houghton did a fantastic job with the final cover design and finished artwork and I am grateful for her time and talent.

Thanks to Ben Parker, the Director of Youth Ministry at Good News and my partner in ministry, for his support and encouragement to get this project done.

Richard Swartley, author of *A Wolf in the Pulpit* (2011), pointed me to Create Space, amazon.com's self-publishing channel. Thank you Richard, I am indebted.

I have tried to give appropriate credit where due throughout the book for the ideas and quotes that have impacted me. If I have neglected to properly attribute an idea or a quote, I apologize and welcome any help in identifying the correct authors and sources for future editions

Finally I thank my wife Deb for being my Number One Cheerleader—*"You should write a book on this!"* I love doing life with you.

I very much appreciate all of this kind and generous support that has enhanced the finished product. Of course, any errors are mine. *All glory is His.*

Resting in Him,

Steve

Attleboro, Massachusetts

April, 2011

Forward
to the second edition

When the first edition of *Obeying Jesus* was published in 2011 some of the initial responses were surprise that I talked about "obeying the commands of Jesus" but then totally ignored the single, central and new command by Jesus to "Love one another." I regret missing the opportunity to include this command to "Love one another" the first time around. So this second edition includes a new chapter on loving one another based on the John 13 command.

Another exciting response to the first edition was reports of some using *Obeying Jesus* as a small-group study. So this second edition also includes a few "Digging deeper..." questions added at the end of each chapter to stimulate personal reflection and facilitate group study and discussion.

Only by grace,
Steve
September, 2012

Introduction

Jesus said *"Go and make disciples…teaching them to obey all that I have commanded."* Yet in spite of growing up in a home of Christians, attending church services whenever the lights were on, reading piles of Christian books, listening to untold hours of sermons, conferences, and Bible studies, tapes, CDs and podcasts, radio and TV programs and attending seminary, I don't recall anyone putting it simply or clearly… "#1, To be a disciple of Jesus is to obey the commands of Jesus. And #2, This is what he commanded…"

This book attempts to fill that gap—to outline the commands of Jesus—first, for my own life and also for the lives of all who claim Jesus as Savior and Lord of their life. After all, if I am a follower of Jesus—a disciple—then I should know his commands and be obeying his commands, right? So the first audience is new believers in Jesus.

I trust that this book is also a useful tool for Christ-followers who are "making disciples." Once you've pointed someone to the Savior, once they have repented and believed, then what? *Teach them to obey all that Jesus commanded.* Hopefully this book will help.

May I suggest that you keep your Bible close at hand as you read through the book so that you can make notes, underline key verses, track extended passages, and "examine the Scriptures … to see if (these things are) true" (Acts 17:11).

CHAPTER 1

Important Last Words

"Then the eleven disciples went to Galilee, to the mountain where Jesus had told them to go. When they saw him, they worshiped him; but some doubted. Then Jesus came to them and said, 'All authority in heaven and on earth has been given to me. Therefore go and make disciples of all nations, baptizing them in the name of the Father and of the Son and of the Holy Spirit, and teaching them to obey everything I have commanded you. And surely I am with you always, to the very end of the age.'"[1]

- Matthew 28:16-20

A person's last words are important. My dad had slipped into a coma before he died, and I regret that I didn't hear his last words and that I don't recall exactly what his last words to me were. Of course, at the time, I didn't realize that they would be his last words. I know that they would have been precious and important, no matter what dad had said.

The last words that Jesus shared with the eleven,[2] those men who had followed him for three and a half years around the dusty roads and hillsides of Judea and sat with him along the rocky shores of Galilee—surely those last words to them were precious and important,

---

[1] Scripture quotations throughout are from *The Holy Bible: The New International Version*, (NIV), 1984 edition, unless otherwise noted.

[2] I recognize that technically, the last words of Jesus are found in Acts 1:7, 8. Yet this intimate conversation, recorded for us in Matthew 28 and known to many as "The Great Commission," is surely a significant part of Jesus' last instructions to his closest followers.

memorable and challenging. And surely after the surprise and amazement of the Ascension into heaven, those disciples would have talked among themselves about what they should do next and how they should act on what Jesus had just told them to do...

> ...*Go and make disciples of all nations, baptizing them in the name of the Father and of the Son and of the Holy Spirit, and teaching them to obey everything I have commanded you.*
> - *Matthew 28:19, 20*

Fortunately for us, they were obedient![3] After the Holy Spirit came upon them in power (Acts 2) just as Jesus had promised, they went and they made disciples, baptizing them in the name of the Father, the Son and the Holy Spirit, and they taught those disciples to obey everything that he had commanded. In fact, they have effectively passed on his commands through many generations, many languages and many cultures. And now the commands of Jesus confront us.

The morning after we talked about the idea of "Skin Deep"—our culture's fascination, some would say our culture's obsession, with looks and beauty—at Good News Bible Chapel where I serve as an elder and the Teaching Pastor, one man commented that he was quite surprised that I didn't give everyone a list of *Do's and Don'ts* to follow—what to wear or not wear, tattoos or no tattoos, acceptable hair styles, clothing styles, music styles, stuff like that. So I mentioned on the Good News Blog at gnbc.org that week that lists of *Do's and Don'ts* can make it easy for some people who just want a list, just want easy answers—"Just tell me what to do..." But I also wrote that sometimes our sincere lists of *Do's and Don'ts* miss the whole point—that people are looking at the outer appearance but God is looking at your heart (1 Samuel 16:7); what is called the *inner beauty*. And *that* comment on the Blog about

---

[3] Look at two other related "One-eights" in the New Testament: "First, I thank my God through Jesus Christ for all of you, because *your faith is being reported all over the world!*" (Romans 1:8); "The Lord's message rang out from you not only in Macedonia and Achaia—*your faith in God has become known everywhere!*" (1 Thessalonians 1:8).

focusing on *inner beauty* brought a response from another brother in Christ, John. He wrote...

> Going through scripture over these years, I found *many* do's and don'ts. For example in Matthew chapters 5:17 and running through to chapter 7, verse 20. The entire set of do's and don'ts ends with these words in verse 21...'not everyone who says to me 'Lord Lord' will enter the kingdom of heaven, but he who does the will of my Father who is in heaven will enter...' Now if Christ did not intend for his disciples to follow these do's and don'ts, why (did he) speak them?

And John is right. The whole Sermon on the Mount in Matthew chapters 5-7 is a one long list of *Do's and Don'ts*: "Do not resist an evil person. If someone strikes you on the right cheek, turn to him the other also." "Love your enemies and pray for those who persecute you," "When you pray, do not be like the hypocrites, for they love to pray standing in the synagogues and on the street corners to be seen by men." And on it goes.

In fact, if you take some time to read through the four gospels—Matthew, Mark, Luke and John—you'll notice that Jesus gave a *lot* of commands. Commands about how to live, how to act, how to spend your money, how to think, how to worship... Depending on how you identify them, and if you count or don't count variations on the same theme, I've found somewhere between 38 and 53 commands of Jesus. (See Appendix A for a complete list.)

Again, in his last words to his disciples just before he ascended to heaven Jesus said...

> All authority in heaven and on earth has been given to me. Therefore go and make disciples of all nations, baptizing them in the name of the Father and of the Son and of the Holy Spirit, *teaching them to obey everything I have commanded you.* And

surely I am with you always, to the very end of the age.

- Matthew 28:18-20

His last words had to be important! His last instructions were "Go and make disciples (the sense of the wording here is "Go, *and as you are going*, make disciples along the way...") of all nations." That word, translated for us from the Greek as "nations," is the word *"ethnos"* from which we get our English word "ethnic." Jesus is not talking here about going to all countries, nations with political borders, but rather he is talking about reaching every ethnic-group—every tribe, every language or tongue, every people group—with the good news of the gospel. "Go," he said, "and as you are going, make disciples along the way of every people group ... baptizing them in the name of the Father and of the Son and of the Holy Spirit, (it's here—verse 20—that I want to focus in this book) *teaching them to obey everything I have commanded you.*"

I suggest at this point that you take some time—maybe on a quiet Sunday afternoon, maybe when you are at the beach or sitting beside the pool on a hot afternoon, maybe when you have a vacation day, or as part of your daily devotions—take some time and read through the four gospels (Matthew, Mark, Luke and John) again. You may have read them before. But this time you're looking for and writing out a list for yourself of every command of Jesus. That would be a simple, practical study, wouldn't it?

In his article, "The Spontaneous Multiplication of Churches"[4] George Patterson teaches from his experience planting churches for 21 years in northern Honduras. "To plant churches in a pioneer field," Patterson writes, "aim for each community to have a group of believers in Christ committed to obey his commands. This definition of a church might get a *D minus* where you studied theology; but the more you add to it, the harder it will be for the churches you start to reproduce. We asked our

---

[4] George Patterson, "The Spontaneous Multiplication of Churches" in *Perspectives on the World Christian Movement: A Reader*, 3rd edition, Winter & Hawthorne, eds. (Pasadena: William Carey Library, 1999), 601.

converts to memorize the following list of Christ's basic commands..." And here Patterson lists seven commands that seem to be the overriding foundational themes of the teaching of Jesus, seven key commands that seem to summarize and include all the other commands.

1. Repent and believe: Mk 1:15
2. Be baptized (and continue in the new life it initiates):
   Mt 28:18-20; Ac 2:38; Rm 6:1-11
3. Celebrate the Lord's Supper: Lk 22:17-20
4. Love God and neighbor in a practical way: Mt 22:37-40
5. Pray: Mt 6:5-15
6. Give: Mt 6:19-21; Lk 6:38
7. Disciple others: Mt 28:18-20

This list is a helpful start for us as believers—both for our own lives as genuine *and obedient* Christ-followers and as effective *and obedient* disciple-makers. Because if we are going to be authentic, sincere disciples of Jesus, it seems that we first need to know just what it is that he has commanded. But, as we begin on this journey, we need to recognize that there is an inherent danger in obeying his commands...

Digging deeper...

● Do you recall the last words of someone who impacted your life? What were they and what do they mean to you now?

● If Jesus had stood next to *you* and said these words to you personally just before he returned to heaven, what would they mean to you today? Would you be living any differently than you are now?

● As you read the commands of Jesus from your own list (or the list at the back of the book) is there anything there that might be God using to get your attention? Write that down here and pray for God to work in you as you read further.

CHAPTER 2

Danger! Danger! Danger!

> *"...if a law had been given that could impart life, then righteousness would certainly have come by the law. ...the law was put in charge to lead us to Christ that we might be justified by faith."*
> *- Galatians 3:21, 23*

Whenever he faced a poisonous snake or a man-eating crocodile, the late Steve Irwin, the energetic and fearless Australian host of Animal Planet's "Crocodile Hunter" cable-TV series, would yell to the camera crew, *"Danger! Danger! Danger!"* He usually had a big grin on his face as he plunged into the water after the crock or pulled the tiny but deadly green viper out of a tree. But Irwin's warnings of danger took on a new and foreboding gravity when he was killed in 2006 by the poisonous barb of a stingray while filming in Australia's Great Barrier Reef.

Likewise, there is a very real danger that comes with focusing on the commands of Jesus. It's called "legalism." The late pastor, author and Bible expositor Ray Stedman taught on legalism and defined it this way: "Legalism is a mechanical and external behavior, growing out of reliance on self, because of a desire to gain a reputation, display a skill, or satisfy an urge to personal power."[5] It is religious performance, religious street theater; posing, scrupulous and meticulous in its outward form that

---

[5] Ray Stedman, "Legalism - Galatians 5:13-23," http://www.raystedman.org/thematic-studies/new-covenant/legalism (Accessed 12/23/2010). Long-time pastor of Peninsula Bible Church in Palo Alto, California, Ray was the pastoral mentor of Luis Palau and Chuck Swindoll.

looks good, that sounds good in its obedience to the commands of Jesus, but, inwardly, as Jesus described it, it's like a "whitewashed tomb"—it looks good on the outside, but it's hiding rot and decay on the inside.

Stedman said that legalism is, first, to have the wrong standard: *to focus on mechanical and external behavior.* And unfortunately, when I have a list of things that I have decided that I should or should not do to be a *good follower* of Jesus, too often the next step is for me to apply *my* list ... *to you*! If I am convinced that I shouldn't go to the local casino, then in no time I'm pretty sure that you shouldn't go to the casino either! If I am convinced that Easter is an evil pagan tradition celebrating the spring solstice, then all too often the next step is to be convinced that *you* shouldn't celebrate Easter either. If I have determined that a glass of wine or a beer is of the devil, then—surprise, surprise —I'm pretty sure the devil drink is bad for *you, too*!

Listen to what the apostle Paul wrote about this in the opening verses of chapter 14 in his letter to the church in Rome: "Accept him whose faith is weak, without passing judgment on disputable matters. One man's faith allows him to eat everything, but another man, whose faith is weak, eats only vegetables." He's talking here about the question of eating meat that had been sacrificed to an idol in a pagan temple and then put out for sale in the meat shop in the temple market area. Verse 3: "The man who eats everything must not look down on him who does not, and the man who does *not* eat everything (that is, the one who has decided that eating meat offered to an idol is just like participating in the worship of an idol, so, it's *obviously* wrong for a Christian to do that) must not condemn the man who does, for God has accepted him." Catch verse 4 here; this is important to our discussion about legalism. "Who are you to judge someone else's servant?" Here he is talking about judging another disciple of Jesus. "Who are you to judge someone else's servant? To his *own* master he stands or falls. And he will stand, for the Lord is able to make him stand."

We had an elder at Good News Bible Chapel for many years, brother Ebben Fennimore. He's in glory now. Ebben was a kind-hearted, gentle and prayerful man. He had decided that Christmas was actually a pagan holiday. So he didn't have a Christmas tree or wish anyone a Merry Christmas. He didn't exchange gifts or send cards. But he never judged anyone who did. He wouldn't "judge someone else's servant." Ebben's convictions were between him and his Lord.

How *will* the Lord make him stand? Listen carefully, this is key, this is *critical* to understanding the gospel: How will the Lord make that meat-eating, Christ follower stand up in honor and righteousness? The answer? By the blood of the cross where the righteousness of Jesus was exchanged for our sin. Where Jesus took all of your sin and shame and where he gave you *his* goodness, gave you *his* right standing before his Father and credited that righteousness to your account. That's 2 Corinthians 5:21: "God made him who had no sin to be sin for us, so that in him *we might become the righteousness of God.*" That exchange—the exchange at the cross of your sin for the righteousness of Jesus—is the core of the good news of biblical Christianity. Miss that, forget that, misunderstand that, and you don't have biblical Christianity.

Stedman observed that legalism is, first, to have the wrong standard: to focus on mechanical and external behavior. Second, he pointed out that legalism has the wrong power: it is "growing out of reliance on ourselves;" what *I* can do, how *I* can act—it is relying on self, the strength of my personality, my upbringing or background, my training or education, my talent or skill, my self-control or self-discipline instead of submitting to and depending on the Spirit of God working in me and through me.

Listen, the flesh, the outer person, the self-disciplined person can teach Sunday School and look great. The flesh can lead worship and look great. The flesh can preach a sermon and sound great. The flesh can go on a missions trip and perform great. The flesh can do *all* of that and ... and it is *nauseating* to God. Why? Because it is done in my own power and not out of total submission, total dependence on the power of the indwelling Christ whom I claim to serve.

Again, the apostle Paul wrote about this to the churches in the province of Galatia, in what is modern day Turkey. In Galatians 2:20 he wrote "I have been crucified with Christ and I no longer live, but Christ lives in me. (What's that? When Jesus died, I died to my old self and have been born again as a ... new creation.) I have been *crucified* with Christ and *I* no longer live, but *Christ lives in me*. The life I live in the body, I live by faith in the Son of God, who loved me and gave Himself for me."

So it's not up to me to try harder, to work harder at being good, but rather it's submitting to the Lordship of Christ in my life: putting Jesus on the throne and I step down and serve instead of leading. That is why we need to recognize the subtlety of all this legalism stuff and to be aware that God looks not at the outward appearance, as man does, but at the inner heart. What is going on inside is all-important to God.

And then third, Stedman made clear that legalism is for the wrong purpose—*"operating for and on behalf of one's own personal glory"*—legalism is following rules that somehow make *me* look good, it focuses on what people think of *me*. I've got to admit, this is tough for me to write about. Because if there is anything about me that is tempted by legalism, by the shiny and spiffy outward appearances of legalism, it is my pride, how people see me, what they think of me.

But in fact, just the opposite is required. We need humility; first, to be willing to be taught by the pressing truth of God's Word. In his book *Instruments in the Redeemer's Hands*, Paul Tripp observes "If I am going to see myself clearly, I need to hold the mirror of God's Word in front of me."[6] Be teachable.

The second God-sent aid in growing in humility is the promised convicting power of the Holy Spirit within us—when you feel that prompting by the Spirit to move away from a habit or a choice or a relationship. My daughter Meegan was wrestling with a decision and she finally said that "The whisper of the Spirit became a scream." Be listening.

The third tool that God uses to make us aware of our legalism is our sisters and brothers in Christ. Hebrews 3:12 and 13 tell us "See to it, brothers and sisters, that none of you has a sinful, unbelieving heart that turns away from the living God. But encourage one another daily, as long

---

[6] Paul David Tripp, *Instruments in the Redeemer's Hands*. (Phillipsburg, NJ: P&R, 2002), 54.

as it is called 'Today,' so that none of you may be hardened by sin's deceitfulness."So we need to listen up when a sister or brother in Christ says "Can we talk for a few moments about something that I'm observing in you?" Be walking in community.

I got a phone call a while back. Chris, a brother whom I deeply respect asked if he could come over to our house and talk with me about something. He sat on the couch in our family room and gently pushed back on me about an attitude he had observed in me on a couple of occasions—an attitude that he admitted he struggles with himself—and he challenged me to examine myself and see if what he was saying was true and if so, to ask the Lord to deal with that attitude in me. I could only thank him for his gentle boldness. I could receive his rebuke because I trusted that his motives were pure—he clearly cared about me and had my best interest at heart; he clearly wanted God to be glorified in me and he didn't want to see me to mess up with my prideful attitude.

In his book *Humility: True Greatness*, C. J. Mahaney observes from his own experience, "On our own, you and I will never develop a competency for recognizing our sin. We'll always need help."[7]

C. J. continues: "Never forget that others see what you do not. Where you are blind to sin, their vision is often twenty-twenty. And by God's grace they can help protect you from the hardening effects of sin. Others can exhort you, encourage you and correct you. They are a gift from God in your battle against sin. And you never grow out of this need. Never."

The question is this: Whose glory are you looking to celebrate with your list of *Do's and Don'ts*? If we're going to spend the next few hours in this book looking at and learning to begin obeying the commands of Jesus—how can we keep that from becoming phony, two-faced, hypocritical legalism—a whitewashed tomb that's shiny clean on the outside ... rotting and stinking on the inside?

That's the challenge as we study the seven commands for every disciple together. It's my challenge; your challenge, to be obedient and yet authentic and genuine. To be humble and teachable. To be

---

[7] C. J. Mahaney, *Humility: True Greatness*, (Colorado Springs: Multnomah Books, 2005), 133.

submissive to the Lordship of the indwelling Christ. To be dependent on the power of the indwelling Spirit. To be focused on giving glory to God, not yourself.

Digging deeper...

- Steadman said that legalism is first, "To have the wrong standard: to *focus on mechanical and external behavior*" (pg. 8). Write out your understanding of legalism in your own words.

- Where do you see that legalism in your life? Write it out here.

- What are you going to do about it? Write it out here.

- Assignment: Turn your desire to give glory to God through your life into a prayer. Write that prayer out and say it every day this week.

CHAPTER 3

Command #1:
Repent & Believe

After John was put in prison, Jesus went into Galilee, proclaiming the good news of God. 'The time has come,' he said. 'The kingdom of God is near. Repent and believe the good news!'

- Mark 1:14 & 15

In the Great Commission of Jesus that we find in Matthew chapter 28, verses 18-20, Jesus told the eleven disciples just before he ascended back to heaven "All authority in heaven and on earth has been given to me. Therefore go and make disciples of all nations, baptizing them in the name of the Father and of the Son and of the Holy Spirit, and teaching them to obey everything I have commanded you..."

These were Jesus' last commands, his last words to his disciples. In Jesus' day, Rabbis—that's what they called their religious teachers, Rabbi—in Jesus' day Rabbis would choose their disciples (or learners, the followers of the Rabbi's disciplines) very carefully because these students were the ones who would pass on the teachings of the Rabbi.

Ray Vander Laan[8] explains that the particular interpretation or understanding of the 613 Mitzvah[9] of the Jewish law that a Rabbi taught

---

[8] Ray Vander Laan, *In the Dust of the Rabbi* (DVD), Faith Lessons Vol.6. (Grand Rapids: Zondervan, 2006).

[9] A "Mitzvah" is a commandment of the Law of Moses given by God to the Israelites at Mount Sinai in Genesis chapter 20 and following. Today when a Jewish boy turns 13 and has a "Bar Mitzvah" ceremony at his Synagogue, he is publically announcing that he is a "Son of the Law," and is bound from that day forward to keep all 613 commands of the Law of Moses. Likewise, a Jewish girl in some circles, upon turning 12 has a "Bat Mitzvah" ceremony, publically declaring

to his followers was called that Rabbi's "yoke." Not like the yoke of an egg; rather like the yoke that holds two oxen together when they pull a plow. The wood yoke locks those two oxen together. Farmers train up a young ox by putting it in the yoke with a strong, well-trained, mature ox. The stronger, well-trained ox bears most of the weight of the yoke and the plow, while the young ox learns how to pull the plow and follow the commands of the farmer by being yoked together with the mature ox.[10]

So the teachings of a Rabbi were called the "yoke" of the Rabbi. It was the yoke or teachings of the Rabbi that tied the student, the follower, the disciple, to that Rabbi. Some Rabbis had long, complex instructions, long lists of *Do and Avoid* that took their disciples years to learn and master. The yoke of many Rabbis could be difficult for their disciples to learn and even tougher for them to obey.

But Jesus said "Take *my* yoke upon you and learn from me, for I am gentle and humble in heart, and you will find rest for your souls" (Mt 11:29). And, he continued, "My yoke is easy and my burden is light." Instead of being a difficult burden, heavy to bear and tough to live out, the teachings of Jesus, the commands that Jesus gives to his followers are easy and his burden is light and when we take up the yoke of Jesus—the commands of Jesus—we will actually find rest for our souls.

People are struggling with the burdens of life. Some are trying to keep their job. Others are trying to handle their health. Some are trying to hold their family together while others are trying to manage their finances, or trying to maintain their relationships. And others are struggling under the burden of "spirituality," trying hard to please God, trying harder to maintain a relationship with God. And Jesus said, "Take

---

that she is now a "Daughter of the Law." In the centuries following the giving of the Law at Mount Sinai, the Jewish Rabbis have added interpretations and oral traditions to the original Law explaining the details and circumstances under which those Laws should be kept, in effect creating a complex list of things to do and things to avoid. Thus for an "observant," or faithful and devout Jew, "Doing and avoiding" become central to "keeping the Law" of Moses. Understanding Mitzvah and the role they play in the life of an observant Jew is critical to understanding both the teachings of Jesus and of the Apostle Paul. See Paul's letter to the Galatians for a closer look at the purpose and limits of keeping the Law of Moses.

[10] Dwight Pentecost, *Design for Discipleship*, (Grand Rapids: Zondervan, 1971), 27-28

my yoke—follow my commands—and you will find rest[11] for your soul." There is peace and rest in following Jesus. As a deeply loved child of God, he has his glory *and* your best interest at heart. And when you obey his commands—they might be pretty radical and counter-cultural—but when you obey his commands, you will find rest for your soul.

In the first chapter I challenged you to begin reading through the four gospels—Matthew, Mark, Luke and John—and begin to make a list of all the commands of Jesus. Some say they have found a hundred! How did you make out in your study? I encourage you to keep on reading, keep on making a list. It will be an easy but very profitable study that will begin to shape the way you see your relationship with Jesus Christ, begin to see him as not just your Savior but also as the Lord of your life who wants you to follow him closely.

In this book we're going to focus on the list of seven key commands that George Patterson distilled from the long list of the commands of Jesus. The first command is in the gospel authored by Mark, known to his friends as John-Mark; he was a cousin of the Apostle Paul's associate, Barnabas. Mark wasn't one of the original disciples, but he was the traveling companion of the Apostle Peter who was an eyewitness of the life and teaching of Jesus and an eyewitness to the resurrection of Jesus. So Mark apparently wrote down the account of the life and teachings of Jesus that he learned directly from Peter.

Mark 1:14 and the following verses tell us "After John was put in prison, Jesus went into Galilee, proclaiming the good news of God. 'The time has come,' he said. 'The kingdom of God is near. Repent and believe the good news!'" Here's the context (Coaching note: always read enough to understand the context): This is the very beginning of the public ministry of Jesus. The gospel by Matthew tells us in chapter 3 that Jesus

---

[11] "Rest" is from the Greek, v. *anapauo* (an-ap-ow'-ō) which means "To refresh, rest up," but also "To cease from labor; to keep quiet, of calm and patient expectation" My desire is to help Christ-followers to learn to rest in the confidence that what Jesus did on the cross for them is *enough.* See J. Hampton Keathley III in the article "The Call To Discipleship: An Invitation To Rest." (http://bible.org/article/call-discipleship-invitation-rest-matthew-1128-30. Accessed: 9/15/2010).

had already been baptized by John the Baptist in the Jordan River, the voice from heaven had boomed out God the Father's intimate, eternal relationship with Jesus and his high approval of Jesus' ministry—"This is my Son, whom I love! With him I am well pleased!"

Right after his baptism, Matthew chapter 4 tells us that Jesus was led by the Spirit into the wilderness for 40 days of prayer and fasting where he was tempted by the devil. And immediately after his temptation, Jesus began his public preaching, "proclaiming the good news of God. 'The time has come,' he said. 'The kingdom of God is near! *Repent and believe the good news!*'"

So the first command of the teaching of Jesus, the first command that his followers need to know and obey is right here: "Repent and believe!"

The word "repent" (Gr. *metanoeo* - pronounce it "met-an-o-eh'-o") in this verse means to change your mind; to stop thinking one way and begin to think in a totally new and different way, to be transformed. Jesus said that to be a Christ-follower means first, to repent, to change your mind. But a Christ-follower needs to ask the question: change your mind about what?

First, change your mind about sin. Too often we think of our sin as a mistake, an unfortunate mistake—but just a mistake, a shortcoming, a character flaw, a weakness, a disease, a genetic defect, an error in judgment ... just about anything *but* seeing our sin as an offense to the sparkling purity, the spotless cleanness of God's holiness. Too often we compare ourselves to someone else (usually conveniently selecting a good example of bad behavior)—"Well, I'm not as bad as_____!"

But when compared to the transcendent and majestic holiness of God, even the good that we do falls short of his perfect standard. The old prophet Isaiah puts it this way: "All of us have become like one who is unclean, and all our righteous acts are like filthy rags (the Hebrew here is actually referring to dirty, stained menstrual cloths! *Eeww!*)—all our best righteous acts are like *filthy rags*; we all shrivel up like a leaf, and like the wind our sins sweep us away" (Isaiah 64:6).

Our no-fault, feel-good-about-myself, "Chopra & Oprah" culture that explains and excuses and tolerates just about any and every behavior has infiltrated our minds and quickly minimizes anything that might be remotely considered sin—and Jesus says *"Enough of that!* Change your mind about that! Start to see your sin the way *I* see your sin—offensive and filthy. Repent! Change your mind!"

If you are a Christ-follower, a disciple of Jesus, you need to see your sin the way God sees your sin. And Jesus said in Matthew 3 that if you genuinely repent, if you really change your mind about your sin and see your sin the way that God sees your sin, you will produce the fruit of repentance, the evidence that you now have the same perspective on your sin as God does.

Listen, if you are still making excuses for a habit that you know offends God, if you are still explaining why it's not your fault about that behavior—"My genes made me do it, it's human nature, I had this craving, everyone does it!"—if you are still thinking that your angry or your unforgiving or your *you-fill-in-the-blank* attitude is somehow justified, then you are not seeing it the way God sees it!

Face it. It's *that* habit that put Jesus on the cross! It's that behavior that stinks before God! Repent! Change your mind about it! See it the same way that God sees it! Turn from it and start producing the fruit of repentance. When we finally begin to see just how broken and wrecked we are by sin, it drags us to the foot of the cross where Jesus died. And there we finally realize that we desperately, hopelessly need a savior. And Jesus says "Repent and believe!" Now, the question is "Believe what?"

Believe that our sin wrecks our relationship with the holy God and that only the death of Jesus—the one and only sinless Son of God—in our place on the cross is enough to satisfy God's demands for punishment for that sin.

Believe, first, that you need a savior. Until you and I know and accept just how holy God is and how lost we are, just how wrecked we are, just how broken and imperfect we are—then we won't understand our need for a savior. Until your friends know just how holy God is and how lost they are, just how wrecked they are, just how broken and imperfect they are—then they won't understand their need for a savior.

First, believe that you need a savior. Second, believe that Jesus is the Son of God who is the way—the *only* way—to a relationship with his Father. The three-and-a-half year public ministry of Jesus was all about drawing people to God the Father through Jesus the Son. So Jesus said "I am the way, the truth and the life; no one comes to the Father except through me!" (John 14:6). There is no *other* way, "no other name under heaven given to mankind by which we must be saved" (Acts 4:12). It is Jesus and Jesus *only*! It is Jesus plus nothing—not sincerity. Not Jesus plus good efforts. Not Jesus plus family coattails. Not Jesus plus church membership or good attendance. Jesus and Jesus alone saves.

In our culture of tolerance and multiculturalism some want us to believe that there are many ways to God and it is rude or arrogant or imperialist to insist that there is only one way. "Just be sincere," they say. Well, Jesus is either the way to a relationship with the Father as he claimed to be—or he is a liar. He said he is the way—that no one comes to the Father except through him.

Unfortunately, many sitting in Bible-teaching churches —many who claim to be born-again Christ-followers—believe that there are many ways to God. They are afraid to suggest to their friends or their family that Jesus is the one and only way. Yet that is what Jesus claimed, that is what he plainly and clearly said. You can't re-write it, you can't modify it or edit the words of Jesus to say and mean something else and still have the message of Jesus. It may be the message of Oprah. It may be the message of your yoga teacher. It may be the language of your World Religions professor. But it is not the message of Jesus.

When Christian Smith and his fellow researchers with the National Study of Youth and Religion at the University of North Carolina at Chapel Hill took a close look at the religious beliefs held by American teenagers, they found that the faith held and described by most adolescents came down to something the researchers identified as "Moralistic Therapeutic

Deism."[12] As described by Smith and his team, Moralistic Therapeutic Deism consists of beliefs like...

1. A god exists who created and ordered the world and watches over human life on earth.
2. God wants people to be good, nice, and fair to each other, as taught in the Bible and by most world religions.
3. The central goal of life is to be happy and to feel good about oneself.
4. God does not need to be particularly involved in one's life except when God is needed to resolve a problem.
5. Good people go to heaven when they die.

After conducting more than 3,000 interviews with American students, the researchers reported that, when it came to the most crucial questions of faith and beliefs, many adolescents responded with a shrug and "whatever." Smith writes "When a young adult says, 'I believe there is a God and stuff,' this hardly represents a deep theological understanding or personal spiritual commitment." Teenagers are not quite as inarticulate about other things. As the researchers found, "Many students know abundant details about the lives of favorite musicians and television stars or sports heroes, about what it takes to get into a good college, but most are not very clear on who Moses and Jesus were."

This study indicated that American young adults are heavily influenced by the ideology of individualism that has so profoundly shaped the larger culture. This bleeds over into a reflexive non-judgmentalism and a reluctance to suggest that anyone might actually be wrong in matters of faith and belief.   Yet Smith reports that "These teenagers are unable to live with a full-blown relativism. They have

---

[12] Christian Smith, "On 'Moralistic Therapeutic Deism' as U. S. Teenagers' actual, tacit, *de facto* religious faith," from *Soul Searching: The Religious and Spiritual Lives of American Teenagers* by Christian Smith with Melinda Lundquist Denton, (Oxford: Oxford University Press, Inc., 2005). Accessed 12/22/2010 at http://www.ptsem.edu/iym/ lectures/2005/ Smith-Moralistic.pdf

strong opinions about what is right and fair. They have very strong opinions about justice. But they seem to be reluctant to go there with matters of faith." And these young adults are no different than the rest of us. Too often we adopt the prevailing mindset of the culture around us including the mindset that minimizes sin and the need for a savior. Moralistic Therapeutic Deism has no need for Jesus, no need for the cross where Jesus died. It might sound good, but Moralistic Therapeutic Deism is not the Historic faith of the apostles, it is not the orthodox faith of the early church, it is not faithful biblical Christianity.

Jesus said that we need to repent—change our mind about our sin; and believe, believe that we need a savior and that Jesus is the only one who saves. Repentance and belief, they're the first steps, the opening chapter of a saving relationship with the living savior, Jesus Christ. I want to stop for a moment and talk with you, as if it were just you and me, alone here in a conversation. Consider for a moment that through his Word, Jesus is speaking directly to you, calling *you* to repent and believe. It is too easy for you and me to think we're pretty good people—especially those of us who were brought up in Christian homes, have been sitting in church Sunday after Sunday for years—and by comparing ourselves to others to be subtly fooled into thinking we're not too bad. But Jesus is speaking to you and to me and he says firmly "Repent of that! Turn from that thinking! See yourself—maybe for the first time—as God the Father sees you and me; as a sinner in need of a savior!"

Jesus says, "Repent ... and believe." Believe that his death on the cross in your place is enough to satisfy the rightly deserved wrath of his holy Father. Believe that Jesus is the Son of God who died in your place and rose again from the grave. Believe that God loves you deeply and wants to make you his child. No coattails. No holding onto sincerity or some sort of silly goodness. Repent of that. Repent and believe that the death of Jesus on the cross in your place is enough. Give up all the other stuff, turn from that, and find peace and rest in what Jesus did for you.

Maybe you have already repented of your sin and have at some time in the past trusted Jesus as your savior. Jesus is calling you today too.

Calling you to repent—to change your mind about the sin that you're holding on to and see it the way he sees it—the sin that put him on the cross. Repent of the attitudes of goodness that make you live through the day like you don't really, desperately need him. Repent of your independence and practical atheism and believe not just the historical facts of the cross and the empty tomb but the reality of living the crucified life with Jesus day by day.

Digging deeper...

- Since repenting means to "Change your mind about sin," what habits/sins do you need to "change your mind" about and start to see from God's perspective? Name them here...

- Do you believe in Jesus? Take a few minutes to think about and write out your "1 Minute Elevator Talk" testimony telling how God saved you. Focus on three things in your "Before & After Story"—first, who you were *before* God saved you; second, what happened at that moment God saved you; and third, who you are now that God has saved you.
  Include two key elements in your story: your understanding of the death of Jesus on the cross in your place, and, include a favorite Bible verse that underlines your faith. Write it all out word for word on a separate piece of paper. Edit it down to sharpen the story and keep it to one minute!

- Assignment: Write out two of the following verses on a card, stick a copy on your bathroom mirror, one over the kitchen sink, one on your car dashboard and put a copy in your pocket. Then memorize them with the text "address" so that you know them cold: Isaiah 59:2; Romans 3:23 & 6:23; Romans 5:6-8; Romans 10:9; Ephesians 2:8&9.

CHAPTER 4

Command #2:
Be Baptized

> *"Therefore go and make disciples of all nations, baptizing them in the name of the Father and of the Son and of the Holy Spirit..."*
> *- Matthew 28:19*

In his last words to his disciples, Jesus told them to go, and as they were going, to make disciples of all nations (Gr. - *ethnos*) i.e., all ethnic-groups, all people groups. We get the first general instruction: *"Go..."* All Christ followers are first commanded by Jesus to step outside their own comfort zone, their own little world and "Go..."

Second, they are to *"make disciples..."* And then we get Jesus' short, two-part explanation of what it means to make disciples; the two basic elements of how to instruct and coach new followers of Jesus; the two foundational elements of discipleship—of following Jesus. The first foundational element of discipleship is, "baptizing them in the name of the Father, the Son and the Holy Spirit..." The second element follows right there: "...teaching them to obey everything I have commanded you."

What happens right after "Repent and believe!"? In the life of someone who has begun to see their sin the way that God sees their sin, has repented—turned from—their sin, recognized their need for a savior, and believed that Jesus is the Son of God, sent from heaven to die on the cross in their place, totally paying the price for their sin—what's next? *I repented, I believe in Jesus. Now what?*

Matthew 28:19 tells us that next step in discipleship for followers of Jesus is to *be baptized*. According to the Bible, being baptized is not about becoming a member of a church. Being baptized does not save you. It's not about a sacred ritual or sacrament for receiving God's grace—though there are churches all around us that teach these things. No, the disciples who heard Jesus give that command to baptize in the name of the Father, the Son and the Holy Spirit would have understood that baptism is first and foremost about "public identification with Jesus and his teaching," to be publically baptized as a follower of Jesus to let everyone in the community know that you were identifying yourself with the message that he preached. There was no such thing as a private baptism, a secret baptism. It was a public event of identification.

Baptism was not invented by Jesus. It was actually pretty common in the first century AD. If you wanted to convert to Judaism, you first were *baptized*—which for Jews was a ritual that symbolized washing away the impurity/uncleanness of your former life as you began a new life in the Jewish faith. So Jews understood the practice of baptism. Remember, Jesus himself was baptized by John, the last of the Old Testament prophets, frequently known as John the Baptist, though I like to call him "John the Witness" because he gave witness to Jesus as the Son of God. In the fall of 2009, my wife Deb and I got to visit the place on the Jordon River where scholars think Jesus was baptized by John. It was evening and getting dark when we got there. The river was cold and quite narrow, just south of where it leaves the Sea of Galilee. There were many fish, visible just under the surface. It was very possibly there, at the beginning of his public ministry, that Jesus went down into the Jordan River before a crowd of onlookers and was baptized by John, publically identifying with the message that John was preaching: "People need to repent, turn away from their sin and turn to God" (Matthew 3:1-13).

And as his own public ministry unfolded, new disciples and followers of Jesus were baptized. The gospel by John, chapter 4, tells us that "The Pharisees (the ultra-religious, law-keeping people of Jesus day) heard that Jesus was baptizing more disciples than John; although in fact it was not Jesus who baptized, but his disciples..." People were publically identifying themselves with the message that Jesus was teaching. After his death on the cross—specifically, after his burial and resurrection—the baptism of followers of Jesus took on a new, deeper and richer meaning. Now it was not just publically identifying with the teaching of Jesus, it also meant that the Christ-follower was publically identifying with the death, the burial and the resurrection of Jesus and all that that meant.

In his letter to the church in Rome (6:3), the apostle Paul writes: "Don't you know that all of us who were baptized into Christ (that is the way that the apostle Paul puts it: when we are baptized, we are baptized *into* Christ) we were baptized into his death? We were therefore buried with him, through baptism into death in order that, just as Christ was raised from the dead through the glory of the Father, we too may live a new life."

Baptism is a powerful symbol; a powerful picture of what happened the moment that we believe in Jesus as our savior. Paul says that when we are baptized, we are publically declaring for everyone to see that "When Jesus died on the cross for my sin, in my place, I was there, I died with Christ." In Galatians, chapter 2, verse 20, Paul writes "I have been crucified with Christ and I no longer live but Christ lives in me..." When a Christ-follower goes under the water, it is like they died and have been buried. And when they come up out of the water, it is a simple but powerful and moving picture of being raised again—just like Jesus was raised from the dead—to begin a new life.

The Greek word *bap-tiz-ō* that is translated as "baptize" in English simply means "to dip, to immerse, to dunk." It is used not only in the Bible but it is the same common Greek word used in everyday manuscripts that archeologists have found dating from Jesus' day that talk about *dipping* fabric in dye and *dunking* cucumbers into pickling solution or a ship *sinking* in battle. The idea is to dip, plunge, dunk, immerse; to submerge under the water and then lift up again. So when we baptize someone as a believer in Jesus, we dip, dunk, immerse, submerge them in water, just as Jesus was dunked by John, just as his disciples would submerge new disciples in water. And we baptize believers in Jesus who are giving public declaration that they have chosen to identify with Jesus, to believe in Jesus, to follow Jesus, the one who died, was buried and rose again.

Now I know that many have been baptized as infants. The Roman Catholic Church teaches that infant baptism is a sacrament by which you receive God's grace and wash away original sin. And some Protestant churches also practice infant baptism—for example, the Episcopal Church, many Presbyterian churches, and others see infant baptism as a rite of initiation into the Christian faith that is similar to infant circumcision for Jewish boys, with adults speaking on the part of the infant. But the example we see in the life of Jesus himself, in the practice of the disciples of Jesus, in the narrative stories in the book of Acts about the infant church—they all speak of people who have made a choice themselves. They *have made a decision to identify with Jesus* and want to declare that decision publically, to tell everyone that they have decided to believe in Jesus as their savior. The church historian, Philip Schaff, writes in his *History of the Christian Church* that baptism of believers was the norm for the first three centuries of the early church. Only later did the practice of infant baptism become common.

> In reviewing the patristic doctrine of baptism ... we should remember that during the first three centuries, and even in the age of Constantine, adult baptism was the rule, and that the actual conversion of the candidate was required as a condition before administering the sacrament (as is still the case on missionary ground). ... But when the same high view is applied without qualification to infant baptism, we are confronted at once with the difficulty that infants cannot comply with this condition. They may be regenerated (this being an act of God), but they cannot be converted, *i.e.,* they cannot repent and believe, nor do they need repentance, having not yet committed any actual transgression. Infant baptism is an act of consecration, and looks to subsequent

instruction and personal conversion, as a condition to full membership of the church. Hence confirmation came in as a supplement to infant baptism.[13]

So we talk about "believers' baptism," as opposed to infant baptism—the baptism of believers in Jesus. If you are a believer in Jesus, if you are trusting Jesus and Jesus only to save you, then Jesus said that you need to make a public announcement, a public confession and display of your faith by being ... baptized. A lengthy public testimony is not required by the text. It is simply to say "I believe that Jesus is the son of God who died for my sin, was buried and rose again to save me." And based on that testimony, Christ-followers are to be baptized, Jesus said, in the name of God the Father, the Son and the Holy Spirit—the Trinity.

If you are a follower of Jesus and you haven't been baptized as a believer in Jesus, the first step of obedience in your life as a disciple of Jesus is to be baptized. You may be a new believer. You may have been a believer for many years. You may have already been baptized as an infant. But obeying the commands of Jesus calls you to make a public declaration of your faith by being baptized it the name of the Father, the Son and the Holy Spirit. Some people are pretty outgoing, pretty *public* in their personality, and for others, their faith is very personal. If that's *you*, let me challenge you to consider that your faith may be *very* personal, but faith in Jesus is not meant to be *private*. For all disciples of Jesus, to be "Obeying Jesus"—for your faith to be obedient faith in the one you say that you are trusting—then you should be publically baptized as a *believer* in Jesus. Baptism is the first step of obedience to the commands of Jesus.

---

[13] Phillip Schaff (1819-1893), *History of the Christian Church*, (Peabody, MA: Hendrickson Publishers, 3rd edition, July 1, 2006), Chapter 5, "Christian Worship," Section 71, "The Doctrine of Baptism," see Notes.

Digging deeper...

● Baptism is a powerful symbol; a powerful picture of what happened the moment that we believe in Jesus as our savior. Explain in your own words what baptism means in the Bible and what it means to you personally.

● What verse in the Bible do you base that on? Write it out here...

● So have you been baptized as a believer in Jesus yet? Why? Or why not? Is there any reason why you won't be baptized as soon as possible? Write out your thoughts here...

CHAPTER 5

"Dead man walking"

"Don't you know that all of us who were baptized into Christ Jesus were baptized into his death? We were therefore buried with him through baptism into death in order that just as Christ was raised from the dead through the glory of the Father,
we too may live a new life."
- Romans 6:3 & 4

I have repented, I believe, I was baptized... *now what?*

I mean, my sins—past, present, and future—are all forgiven, covered by the blood of Jesus Christ, shed for me on the cross. I have received the mercy and grace of God. I'm on the way to heaven. I believe all that. So what? Look at the apostle Paul's letter to the Christians in Rome, Romans chapter 6, verse 1...

> What shall we say, then? Shall we go on sinning so that grace may increase? By no means! We died to sin; how can we live in it any longer? Or don't you know that all of us who were baptized into Christ Jesus were baptized into his death? We were therefore buried with him through baptism into death in order that, just as Christ was raised from the dead through the glory of the Father, *we too* may live a new life.
>
> If we have been united with him like this in his death, we will certainly also be united with him in his resurrection. For we know that our old self was crucified with him so that the body of sin might be done away with, that we should no longer

be slaves to sin—because anyone who has died has been freed from sin.

Now if we died with Christ, we believe that we will also live with him. For we know that since Christ was raised from the dead, he cannot die again; death no longer has mastery over him. The death he died, he died to sin once for all; but the life he lives, he lives to God.

In the same way, count yourselves dead to sin but alive to God in Christ Jesus. Therefore do not let sin reign in your mortal body so that you obey its evil desires. Do not offer the parts of your body to sin, as instruments of wickedness, but rather offer your-selves to God, as those who have been brought from death to life; and offer the parts of your body to him as instruments of righteousness."

If you are trusting in God's grace and mercy shown at the cross in the death of Jesus for you—if you believe and have been baptized—then your baptism was symbolic of you dying when Christ died and you rising to new life just as Christ rose from the grave.

So, the apostle Paul is saying, if that's you—*then live the new life*! The redeemed life! The regenerated life! The resurrected life! Galatians 6:14 tells us "May I never boast except in the cross of our Lord Jesus Christ, through which the world has been crucified to me, and I to the world." "Set your minds on things above, not on earthly things. For you died, and your life is now hidden with Christ in God" (Colossians 3:2,3).

Over and over Paul tells us that to die with Christ means to be dead to the worldly system around us, to be dead to the power of sin to control you and to be alive to God. Baptism is not the goal, not the end—it is just publicly announcing the *beginning* of new life in Christ!

When Jesus said that his followers are to take up their cross daily and follow him, he meant exactly this: dying daily to the impulses of selfishness. Dying daily to the urge and power of sinful habits. Dying daily to the priorities and pace, the passions and perks of a worldly lifestyle. This is called "living the crucified life" from Galatians 5:24

"Those who belong to Christ Jesus have crucified the sinful nature with its passions and desires."[14]

The crucified life is dead to the sins that entangle and enslave us. Dead to worldly lures that distract and discredit us. Dead to selfishness that is idolatry because it replaces God in our lives. Again in Galatians 2:20, Paul says "I have been crucified with Christ and I no longer live, but Christ lives in me. The life I live in the body, I live by faith in the Son of God, who loved me and gave Himself for me." The crucified life is a life not of joyless boredom or super-saintly other-worldness. The crucified life is not rigid religiosity or clueless detachment. No, the crucified life is first a life that notices and appreciates God's grace and mercy every day—and lives in that grace, free of self-condemnation and self-hate and free of judging others.

Second, the crucified life is a cross-centered life that realizes how lost we are without the cross and lives every day humbly in the deep shadow of that cross—refusing to get caught again in patterns and habits that disappoint our Father in heaven and destroy our conversation with him. John Piper writes "Paul was utterly mastered, held captive, by one great scene in history: a cross on Golgotha and on it the Son of God who loved us and gave himself for us."[15] If that is the same picture which captures *your* heart and mind, how can you possibly deliberately choose to sin any longer?

Third, the crucified life is the life that daily realizes the costliness of sin: it was our sin, my sin, your sin, that nailed Jesus to the cross—that brought him public shame and physical pain; that caused his feeling of separation from his Father in heaven. 2 Corinthians 5:21 - "For our sake

---

[14] This is what the Puritan pastor and statesman John Owen (1616-1683) called "mortification" in his book, *On the Mortification of Sinne in Believers* published in 1656. Owen wrote "There is no death of sin without the death of Christ. ... Believers ought to make the mortification of sin their daily business. Indwelling sin always abides; therefore it must always be mortified. Indwelling sin not only abides, but is still acting. It is not only still acting but it will produce more soul-destroying sins if it is not mortified. The life, vigor and comfort of our spiritual life depends much on the mortification of sin because sin, left alone, will deprive us of life, vigor and comfort."

[15] John Piper, quoted by C. J. Mahaney in *Living the Cross Centered Life* (NY: Doubleday, 2006).

he made him to be sin who knew no sin, so that in him we might become the righteousness of God."

Fourth, the crucified life is a life that has killed, executed the *natural self*—the old sin nature—that sits on the throne of your life and installed the living Christ on the throne instead. We read that in Romans 6:6, "For we know that our old self was crucified with him so that the body of sin might be done away with, that we should no longer be slaves to sin…" Oswald Chambers wrote "If we do not purposely sacrifice the natural, the supernatural can never become natural to us." When we come to Jesus, repenting and believing, then the old life is dead, the new life has begun: "Therefore, if anyone is in Christ he is a new creation-- the old has passed, the new has come!" (2 Corinthians 5:17).

The story is told of Augustine of Hippo, the philosopher and theologian living from AD 354 to 430 and one of the leading voices of the early church. He grew up in a comfortable middle-class family and as a young man turned to a life of partying, drinking and pretty wild living. After God saved him, his life was totally transformed. One day, walking down the street, he saw a woman approaching, one of his former mistresses. Augustine turned around and began walking away from her quickly. But she saw him and cried out "Augustine, Augustine, it is I!" And he responded over his shoulder as he kept on speed-walking, "I know, but it is not I!"[16]

Augustine was living the crucified life. He had died to the old man—the old Augustine—and was living a new life. The best way that I know to kill the old man, the old self and its sinful desires, is to starve it to death. Stop feeding it. Stop feeding what makes it possible for sin to live and grow in your mind, in your attitudes and in your actions. If you need to change the friends you hang out with because they influence your decisions (1 Cor 15:33), then start there and get new friends who will be a good influence on you. If you need to eliminate the cable TV channels that are too tempting or they mess with your mind, then do it. Whatever it takes. Jesus called it cutting off what offends:

---

[16] Ambrose, *Concerning Repentance,* 2.10.96, Nicene and Post-Nicene Fathers, 2nd ser., vol. 10 (reprint, Grand Rapids, Mich.: Wm. B. Eerdmans Publishing Co., 1969), p. 357.

You have heard that it was said, 'Do not commit adultery.' But I tell you that anyone who looks at a woman lustfully has already committed adultery with her in his heart. If your right eye causes you to sin, gouge it out and throw it away. It is better for you to lose one part of your body than for your whole body to be thrown into hell. And if your right hand causes you to sin, cut it off and throw it away. It is better for you to lose one part of your body than for your whole body to go into hell. - Matthew 5:27-30

I call that "radical amputation." Of course Jesus was not talking literally but rather with hyperbole; using deliberate exaggeration to make the point: cut off, amputate, totally eliminate whatever is tempting you, teasing you, leading you, causing you to fall into sin.

Baptism is not the end but rather an announcement of the *beginning* of that new life. So the question is, is there something of the old life that is still hanging on in you? Is there something that needs to be crucified in your life today? A habit that has some strange power over you? An attitude that poisons your thinking or your relationships? A priority that has taken the place of loving and serving God? A passion that has taken the place of loving and serving God's people? A joy—or a fear—in your life that has subverted, has pushed out, has taken the place of delight and joy in your relationship with God? Are you still holding onto old religious beliefs or superstitions that need to be executed, need to be nailed to the cross? Are you hanging onto guilt and shame and regret that is keeping you from the joy and freedom of forgiveness and new life in Christ—guilt and shame and regret that needs to be crucified? Are you looking for something in this world—success or recognition, money or stuff, pleasure or pride—that needs to be out to death so that you can live a new life in the shadow of the cross of Christ?

Digging deeper...

- What does "Count yourselves dead to sin but alive to God in Christ Jesus" mean to you?

- Read Matthew 5:27-30 again. What habit do you need to "radically amputate?" Pray about it, name it and write out the first 2 or 3 steps you have to take in this practical, powerful surgery...

- *Assignment:* Write out 1 Corinthians 10:13 on a card, stick it in your pocket, and memorize it cold this week.

CHAPTER 6

Command #3:
"Remember Me"

"After taking the cup, he gave thanks and said, 'Take this and divide it among you. For I tell you I will not drink again of the fruit of the vine until the kingdom of God comes.' And he took bread, gave thanks and broke it, and gave it to them, saying, 'This is my body given for you; do this in remembrance of me.' In the same way, after the supper he took the cup, saying, 'This cup is the new covenant in my blood, which is poured out for you.'"

- Luke 22:17-20

The report by Dr. Luke tells us that on the night that he was betrayed, arrested and put on trial, Jesus met in a quiet upstairs room with his disciples to celebrate the Passover, the annual Jewish feast that recalled the time about 1,400 years earlier when the children of Israel were still living as slaves to Pharaoh in Egypt. You can find the incredible story in Exodus chapters three through twelve. Moses approached Pharaoh and asked him to "Let my people go!" Pharaoh refused. And as promised, ten times God brought plagues on the Egyptians to force Pharaoh to reconsider: The Nile River turned to blood, the land was overrun with frogs, then lice, then flies, then pestilence, then all the people suffered from boils, then the devastating hailstorm came, then whatever wasn't destroyed by the hail was eaten by locusts, then the whole land was covered in darkness, and finally the angel of death flew over the land and every firstborn in every home, from the poorest peasant to the palace of Pharaoh himself, even the first born of the cattle, died. Except in the area of Egypt called Goshen where the Hebrew slaves lived. There God told Moses to have every family take a lamb—it had to be a spotless lamb, no defects or scars, no illnesses or deformities, it had to be a perfect lamb in every way (Exodus 12:5)—and the father of the family had to take that little lamb, kill the lamb and pour out the blood, then paint the blood onto the sides and the top of the door of their house (Exodus 12:7). That night, when the angel of death saw the blood of the lamb on the door frame of the house, the angel of death would *pass over* that house and the first-born child of that family would be saved.

That was the night that Pharaoh finally relented. He let the Hebrew slaves go in their great flight from Egypt. The book of Exodus tells us that they ate their dinner that night with their traveling clothes on, their walking stick in hand, they didn't even take time for the bread to rise but ate bread without yeast, unleavened bread (Exodus 12:8-11), and then headed out on the long trip through the wilderness from Egypt to the promised land.

In Exodus 12 God commanded that every year they remember that night that they were saved, the night when the angel of death had "passed over" the homes where the blood of the innocent lamb had been poured out (Exodus 12:14-20). So each following year every Hebrew family took time to remember how utterly miserable and totally helpless they were in slavery and then how God had rescued them from a life of bondage and slavery and brought them out to deliverance and freedom. Every year, as they ate the Passover dinner together as a family, they would look back and remember the bitterness of being a slave, and the sweet taste of freedom. Every year at the Passover dinner they would remember the little innocent lamb that died as a substitute so that the first-born of that family could live; the spotless lamb that took the place of the one under the threat of death. Every year they looked back and remembered God's mercy and grace, God's great love for them. For over 1,400 years, Jewish people—wherever they were, all over the world—had been remembering the night of the Passover with the Passover dinner.

Jesus chose *that* annual Passover dinner—that meal of remembrance that all Jewish people around the world still share annually to this day—to initiate a *new* dinner, a *new* meal of remembrance, what we today call "The Lord's Supper." Sometimes we call it "Communion" because it is something that we do together as a *community* of God's redeemed, saved people who are in close relationship/communion with each other and in close communion with our Savior. Sometimes we call it "The Eucharist" which simply is the Greek word which means "thanksgiving;" a meal of thanksgiving for the death of Jesus that set us free from the curse of sin and death. Sometimes we call it "Breaking of Bread," the name that the infant church used in the book of Acts for remembering Jesus with the bread and the cup.

There are four instructive parallels between the Passover dinner and the Lord's Supper, Communion, Breaking of Bread. First, we have said that the Passover dinner was a meal of *remembering*. All of the details of the Passover dinner pointed back to the night the angel of death passed over the houses with doors painted with the blood of the lamb. The whole dinner was designed to help the Hebrews remember, and never forget, the night that they were rescued from slavery and set free. In our text in Luke 22, verse 19, Jesus said that night "This is my body given for you; do this in remembrance of me." He chose his words carefully; he made it clear that the meal he was about to command them to repeat was a meal of remembrance. The bread that they shared would help them to remember his body, given as a sacrifice for their sin on the cross. The cup that they shared would help them to remember his blood, shed for the forgiveness of their sins. This uncomplicated meal of a piece of bread and a drink of juice is simply to help us remember, and never forget, the price of our freedom from the power and penalty of sin, the costliness of our salvation, the value to God of our forgiveness—it was nothing less than the body and blood of Jesus Christ, the holy Son of God.

There are some who say that Communion, the Eucharist, the Lord's Supper, is actually an instrument, a channel, a way that you receive God's grace. And others say that something mystical happens when the words of remembrance are recited, that in some miraculous way the bread and wine are transformed into the real body and real blood of Jesus and by taking them we are in very real communion with him. This is taking the common Eastern hypoerbolic style of speaking too literally. So we understand the bread and the cup to be symbolic; just simple but yet powerful symbols of his body and blood, no more. Jesus said that we should remember him with bread and the cup, so that we would never forget.[17]

I don't know about you, but to be honest, my life is pretty busy, maybe as busy as yours. And I know that I need opportunities to remember Jesus and his death on the cross with the bread and cup because if I didn't pause to do that frequently, it's not like I would "forget" about him, but, I wouldn't "remember." Know what I mean? I think Jesus understands. He knows that we're just sophisticated piles of dust; easily distracted by the business and busyness of life. And we'd forget to remember if we didn't have a simple reminder.

The second parallel between the Passover and the Lord's Supper is found in the Passover lamb—a substitute. The lamb took the place of the first-born child. The lamb died so the child would not. In the same way, Jesus was your substitute, bearing the full wrath of God that you—that I—deserve. His death on the cross satisfied the wrath of a holy God against my sin and yours. 1 Peter 3:18 tells us "For Christ died for sins once for all, the righteous for the unrighteous, to bring you to God." And again, Peter wrote "he himself bore our sins in his body on the tree, that we might die to sin and live to righteousness," (1 Peter 2:24). Jesus is the substitute who took my place—your place—and bore the punishment for sin that we deserve.

---

[17] John Calvin writes "What we have so far said of the Sacrament abundantly shows that...it was ordained to be frequently used among all Christians in order that they might frequently return in memory to Christ's Passion, by such remembrance to sustain and strengthen their faith, and urge themselves to sing thanksgiving to God and to proclaim his goodness...." *Institutes of the Christian Religion* John T. McNeill ed., Ford Lewis Battles trans.. Library of Christian Classics (Philadelphia: Westminster, 1960 [1559]) IV.xvii.44, 46

Third, we notice that the Passover lamb had to be spotless, perfect in every way (Exodus 12:5). And Jesus was spotless, perfect in every way; Hebrews 4:15 tells us that he was "one who has been tempted in every way, just as we are—yet was without sin." He was a perfect, spotless sacrifice: "Such a high priest meets our need—one who is holy, blameless, pure, set apart from sinners, exalted above the heavens" (Hebrews 7:26); "God made him who had no sin to be sin for us, so that in him we might become the righteousness of God" (2 Corinthians 5:21). 1st Peter 1:19 tells of "the precious blood of Christ, a lamb without blemish or defect."

Fourth, that first-born Hebrew child in Egypt that night was doomed to die like all of the other first-born in the land, totally helpless and hopeless unless the blood of the lamb was painted on the frame of the door. And because of our broken, fallen, sinful selves, we too are doomed to spiritual death, totally hopeless and helpless without a savior. Romans 5:12 tells us "Therefore, just as sin came into the world through one man, and death through sin, and so death spread to all men because all sinned" (ESV). The good news is that Jesus intervened and offers hope to the hopeless: "But God demonstrates his own love for us in this: While we were still sinners, Christ died for us. ... You see, at just the right time, when we were still powerless, Christ died for the ungodly" (Romans 5:6, 8).

Fifth, it was only the blood of the pure and innocent Passover lamb that made it possible for the angel of death to pass over that household. And it is only the blood that Jesus poured out there on the cross that makes it possible for God to forgive your sin and mine. In fact, Hebrews 9:22 tells us that "without the shedding of blood there is no forgiveness of sin." 1 John 1:7 teaches us that it is "the blood of Jesus Christ that cleanses us from all sin" (see Leviticus 17:11).

But I want to step back from the details and look again at the big picture parallel. We said that like the Passover meal, the Lord's Supper, is all about remembering Jesus and his death on the cross. Did you notice that a priest was not involved in the Passover meal? The night that the Hebrew slaves got ready to escape from Egypt, each family—or, if they were too poor to own a lamb, each group of families—made the sacrifice and shared in the Passover meal together. But no priest was involved. The night that Jesus celebrated the Passover with his disciples, no Jewish priest was involved. He did not tell them that only a priest could officiate at the meal for them. And if we look through the book of Acts at what happened in the early church, we find no sign of a special class of Christian—someone who has a special title, who has a distinct role, who had a special education or wore special clothes—who must lead or officiate at the Lord's Supper.

When we look at Acts chapter 2, beginning in verse 41, we get a snap-shot picture of the infant church in action: "Those who accepted his (Peter's) message were baptized, and about three thousand were added to their number that day." That is pretty incredible! The infant church grew from about 120 believers (Acts 1:15) to 3,000 Christ-followers in one day!

> They devoted themselves to the apostles' teaching and to the fellowship, to the breaking of bread and to prayer. Everyone was filled with awe, and many wonders and miraculous signs were done by the apostles. All the believers were together and had everything in common. Selling their possessions and goods, they gave to anyone as he had need. Every day they continued to meet together in the temple courts. They broke bread in their homes and ate together with glad and sincere hearts, praising God and enjoying the favor of all the people. And the Lord added to their number daily those who were being saved (Acts 2:42-47).

There were no church buildings for this instant "church" to meet in until more than 100 years later. Instead, they met, as many as could attend, in the courtyard of the Jewish Temple. They also met daily in each other's homes. And they *broke bread* together—this phrase "broke bread" is used throughout the New Testament for what we call Communion or the Lord's Supper: "And they devoted themselves to the apostles' teaching and the fellowship, to the breaking of bread and the prayers" (Acts 2:42, ESV); "On the first day of the week we came together to break bread..." (Acts 20:7; see 1 Corinthians 10:16). They broke bread—they remembered the Lord in each other's houses with the bread and the cup. Notice that there is no mention of priests or some special class of Christian officiating at this remembrance meal. The division of Christians into two classes of clergy and laity is not found here in Acts, or anywhere else in the New Testament. Yes, there was a designated priesthood in the Old Testament with special titles, distinctive clothes and distinguishing roles and responsibilities. But in the New Testament paradigm we are all priests unto God under our High Priest, Jesus Christ Himself: "But you are a chosen race, a royal priesthood, a holy nation, a people for his own possession, that you may proclaim the excellencies of him who called you out of darkness into his marvelous light" (1 Peter 2:9; see Revelation 5:10). We are all sisters and brothers in Christ with no distinctions. The early church didn't develop a separate class of "clergy" until the second and third century after Christ.[18] It is obvious and biblical that we have different gifts, different roles and responsibilities (see Romans 12:4-8; 1 Corinthians 12; Ephesians 4:11-13). But before God we are all the same, just sisters and brothers in Christ. That's one reason why I resist being called "Pastor" (Matthew 23:8-10) and prefer to just be called by my name, Steve. While some see "Pastor" as a title of respect, it seems to imply that there is something special or different about me. And such distinctions are too easily, too quickly a source of pride and self-importance, inappropriate attitudes for servants of the Master (Mark 9:35; Philippians 1:1a). I am no different before God than you. You certainly don't need me, or one of the elders to "officiate" for you to be able to break bread to remember the Lord. You have been invited by

---

[18] Tertullian of Carthage at the close of the second century in his paper entitled "On Monogamy" may have been the first to use the word *clerus* in the sense of clergy, writing in chapter 12, "*Unde enim episcopi et clerus?* ..." In English, the passage reads, "For whence is it that the bishops and clergy come?

Jesus himself to remember him with the symbols of his body and blood, bread and the cup, even in your home, even in your small groups.

So first, the Lord's Supper is about remembering Jesus in his death and his resurrection. Second, no special class of Christian is needed to for us to remember the Lord together. Third, the Passover dinner was an annual celebration, an annual feast of remembering. But in 1 Corinthians 11:26 the apostle Paul said *"Whenever* (emphasis mine) you eat this bread and drink this cup, you proclaim the Lord's death until he comes." In fact the early church seemed to do it at least weekly. We already saw in Acts 2 that they broke bread in their homes, apparently daily. In Acts 20 we find the apostle Paul in the city of Troas. Verse 7: "On the first day of the week we came together to break bread. Paul spoke to the people and, because he intended to leave the next day, kept on talking until midnight..." Meeting together on the first day of the week, Sunday, was a break for the new Christians from the Jewish tradition of keeping the Sabbath which for Jews is sundown Friday night until sundown Saturday night. But apparently the church met in homes on the first day of the week, "the Lord's day," (see 1 Corinthians 16:2; Revelation 1:10) and broke bread. Certainly they broke bread to remember the Lord more frequently than the once-a-year celebration of Passover. And certainly it was more frequently than the typical quarterly or even monthly opportunity to remember the Lord that most evangelical churches offer today.

So in our tradition, we are trying at the Good News Bible Chapel to follow what seems to be the example of the early church by meeting every week for Breaking of Bread.[19] We set aside an hour on Sunday

---

[19] It must be recognized and granted that all attempts to reconstruct the life of the first century church in today's time and circumstances suffers immediately and fatally—in spite of frequent claims to the contrary—from a serious paucity of explicit details in Scripture about just how the infant church actually functioned. This disappointing lack of detail is actually a God-ordained blessing, relieving us from slavishly reproducing the form and function of the early church and quickly thinking that our slavish rituals pass for authentic faith and devotion. This lack of instruction in details actually gives us considerable freedom! So for Good News Bible Chapel—or any other church/denomination/movement—to attempt any claim that *"We* are doing it the New Testament way!" would be an absurd and prideful assertion that should always be surfaced and usually rejected wherever it is offered.

morning to focus on remembering Jesus, usually sitting in a square with all the rows of chairs facing into the center where the simple center table is set with the bread and the cup. For example, recently the theme for one particular Lord's day morning was from the book of Revelation chapter 1, verse 17 and 18: "When I saw him, I fell at his feet as though dead. Then he placed his right hand on me and said: 'Do not be afraid. I am the First and the Last. I am the Living One; I was dead, and behold I am alive forever and ever! And I hold the keys of death and Hades.'" A number of different brothers stood and commented on that passage. Others shared from other related scriptures. Dozens of brothers and sisters offered brief personal expressions of praise: "I praise Jesus for..." Some sisters and brothers suggested hymns or choruses that we could sing together. Others led us in prayer. All focused on the person and work of Jesus. I didn't lead the service; in fact, no one led the service. Other than the announced theme text, it wasn't planned or scripted. Each believer who attended was free to participate—or not participate—as the Holy Spirit prompted them. We take the example from Colossians 3:16: "Let the word of Christ dwell in you richly as *you teach and admonish one another* (emphasis mine) with all wisdom, and as you sing psalms, hymns and spiritual songs with gratitude in your hearts to God." That echoes Ephesians 5:19 where Paul wrote: "Speak to one another with psalms, hymns and spiritual songs." Again Paul told the Corinthians "What shall we say then brothers? When you come together, everyone has a hymn, or a word of instruction, a revelation, a tongue or an interpretation. All these must be done for the strengthening of the church" (1 Cor. 14:29). That's the kind of freedom that we try to allow for each week in that remembrance service that culminates in breaking the bread and drinking the cup together. This open, Spirit-led remembrance service is distinctive, something quite different than what you might find in most other churches. I am certainly not saying that we've got it right and other churches don't. That's not the point; it's not about putting any other church traditions down or exalting ours.

What I *am* trying to say is that we're attempting to be obedient to the command of Jesus to "Remember me." To do it more often, not less because we need to be reminded often. To do it simply, with no distinction of special classes of Christians. And to focus simply on remembering Jesus—not on a sacramental ritual, not on a mystical moment when the tiny bell rings—just remembering Jesus. Some mornings this service at Good News is tender and quiet. Sometimes it is loud and joyful and full of praise. Some Sundays there are extended times of silence for reflection and meditation. Other times there's not a quiet moment.

There certainly are other ways to remember Jesus—to be honest, the particular form that we follow at Good News is as much from the tradition of our heritage as from Scripture. For example, the Bible doesn't require it to be an entire service set apart for that purpose. It could be part of a fellowship meal like what we see the early church doing in 1 Corinthians chapter 11. It could be part of your mid-week small group meeting. It could be with your family on the beach during vacation.

The point is that *you* have been invited personally by Jesus himself to a simple symbolic meal to remember him and not forget; to remember his death in your place so that you can be forgiven; to remember his innocent perfectness and remember the violent cost of your redemption; to remember the past and look forward to his soon return. Jesus invites you to remember him with the bread and the cup often.

Digging deeper...

● What do the bread and the cup mean in the Communion/Eucharist/Lord's Supper?

● What bible verses mentioned in this chapter do you base that understanding on? Write out two of those verses here...

● Is it helpful for you to "Remember Jesus more, not less?" If so, what can you do to remember Jesus more? Write out something specific that you can do weekly, monthly, quarterly, annually to remember Jesus more.

CHAPTER 7

Command #4:

Pray

"This, then, is how you should pray:
'Our Father in heaven, hallowed be your name,
your kingdom come, your will be done, on earth as it is in heaven.
Give us today our daily bread.
Forgive us our debts, as we also have forgiven our debtors.
And lead us not into temptation, but deliver us from the evil one."
- Matthew 6:9-13

I heard the story about a hiker out in the wilderness of Alaska, far from nowhere. As he came around a bend on the trail he stopped dead in his tracks. There in front of him was the largest snarling, drooling grizzly bear he'd ever seen. He was terrified. He thought "I've always been an atheist—so it's not really fair, just because I'm in trouble, for me to pray now and ask God to save me." So instead he prayed that God would make the bear a Christian. And just then, the giant grizzly dropped to its knees, put its huge front paws together and began to *pray!* "Dear God, thank you for this food I am about to eat. Amen." Cute.

The *Westminster Shorter Catechism* (answering Question 98) says that "Prayer is an offering up of our desires unto God, for things agreeable to his will, in the name of Christ, with confession of our sins, and thankful acknowledgment of his mercies." Dennis Fuqua writes that prayer is the alignment of our will and desires with God's will and desires.[20] To put it simply, prayer is just talking with God; having a personal conversation with God. I like the scene in *Fiddler on the Roof* where Tevya is trudging along, pulling his cart and his cow behind him, and he's talking to someone. And you slowly realize that Tevya—an Orthodox Jew—is having an ongoing conversation with God. He's explaining, he's arguing, he's angry, he's grateful—it's an ongoing conversation.

How did Jesus pray? When did Jesus pray? Why did Jesus pray? We can learn some lessons about prayer from examining the prayer life of Jesus. But before we look at the prayer life of Jesus, I want to step back for a moment and not assume that we are all starting from the same page or even the same chapter on the subject of prayer. There are lots of different types of prayer that people offer. Some people pray to God. Others pray to dead relatives or even their dead pets. Some pray to trees or the sun. So just to be sure, let's check in with what the Bible teaches when it comes to prayer. After all, the Bible is *the* ultimate source of truth: 2nd Timothy 3:16 teaches us that "All Scripture is God-breathed and is useful for teaching, rebuking, correcting and training in righteousness." So let's ask first what prayer is, and isn't.

I think that the Psalms give us a similar picture of prayer. The Psalms are personal. They're frank and to the point. Sometimes, the psalm writer is excited and happy and joyful. So for example, in Psalm 101 the psalm writer is praying "I will sing of your love and justice; to you, O LORD, I will sing praise." Sometimes the writer is regretful or longing. In Psalm 51 the psalm writer is praying "Create in me a pure heart, O God, and renew a steadfast spirit within me. Do not cast me from your presence or take your Holy Spirit from me. Restore to me the joy of your salvation." Other times, the psalm writer is sad or afraid. Sometimes they call down curses upon their enemies! But in every case, the writers of the psalms are pouring out their thoughts and feelings,

---

[20] Dennis Fuqua, *Living Prayer: The Lord's Prayer Alive in You.* (Self-published, 2010). Available online from http://livingprayerbook.web.officelive.com/BuyNow.aspx

their hopes and anxieties—they're having a conversation with God. That's what prayer is; talking with God.

So if prayer is simply talking with God—telling him what you are thinking and feeling, what is prayer "not?" A look at Matthew chapter 6 shows us a quick teaching on prayer by Jesus; what prayer is and isn't. Look at verse 5. Jesus says "And when you pray..." (Note that he says "when," not "if;" Jesus is expecting his followers to be praying followers) "do not be like the hypocrites, for they love to pray standing in the synagogues and on the street corners to be seen by men. I tell you the truth, they have received their reward in full." So praying is not a chance to show off how religious you are. People might be impressed, but God isn't!

And prayer is not a chance to impress God with your fancy words. God's heard them all before—and fancier than mine or yours. Trust me, he's not impressed. What does impress God is a sincere and humble heart. Psalm 51:17 says "The sacrifices of God (or the sacrifices that please God, that God finds acceptable) are a broken spirit; a broken and contrite heart, O God, you will not despise." Jesus continued in his teaching about prayer in Matthew 6. He said in verse 6 "But when you pray, go into your room, close the door and pray to your Father, who is unseen. Then your Father, who sees what is done in secret, will reward you. And when you pray, do not keep on babbling like pagans, for they think they will be heard because of their many words. Do not be like them, for your Father knows what you need before you ask him." So God is not impressed by many words, by long prayers, by repeated prayers. Jesus called repeating the same words—the same prayers, over and over—"babbling." God is not impressed with how many times you say a prayer.

I know that many come from a church background that has taught you to repeat a memorized prayer over and over. In fact, some have been taught to repeat a prayer over and over many times as a sign of repentance. Jesus says here in Matthew 6:6 that God is not impressed. In fact, the Bible never tells us to repeat a prayer over and over. Would you go to your wife and repeat the same conversation over and over? Would you talk to your boss and say the same things over and over? Do you think she or he would be impressed? God hears your prayer the first time. And Jesus said that God knows your heart, he knows you—Jesus says here in verse 6 that God knows what you need before you even ask him.

Jesus in Matthew 6:9 taught his followers to pray with what is known as the Lord's prayer—some call it "the Disciple's Prayer." Jesus is speaking and he says "This, then, is how you should pray: 'Our Father in heaven...'" This is simply acknowledging who God is, the one that we are dependent on in every way. Notice that Jesus says that our prayer should be addressed to the Father. Not to Jesus, not to the Holy Spirit. Not to a saint. Nowhere in Scripture do we find an example of prayer addressed to anyone except God the Father.

In *Living Prayer* Dennis Fuqua explains that Jesus teaches his disciples—and us—to pray with these words: "Hallowed..." (or holy—set apart, distinct) be your name, Father." Jesus is teaching us to begin our prayer by asking "Let your name be holy, distinct Father here on earth—in my life, in my home, in my work, in my community—the same way that it is holy in heaven."

"Let your kingdom come..." The "Kingdom of God" is where God is king, where he rules and reigns. Jesus said "The kingdom of God is within you" (Luke 17:21). This is praying that God will rule and reign—in me, in my family, in my work, in my community, in my church—the very same way that he rules and reigns in heaven.

"Let your will be done ..." This is praying that the good and perfect plan of God will happen here on earth—in my life, in my home, in my work, in my community—in the same way that the will of God is desired and accomplished in heaven, acknowledging and submitting to the sovereignty of God in my life.

"Give us today our daily bread..." It is interesting to notice that the word "daily" is used only here it the New Testament. It means "sufficient for the day." "Give us today our daily bread"—give us what we need for today. Here's where Jesus is teaching us that it is okay to ask God for the simple things that we need for the day—but notice its simple needs;

bread not cheesecake! And he is teaching us to ask daily, early in the day!

Jesus continues—"Forgive us our debts, as we also have forgiven our debtors." And in case we missed the point, the Holy Spirit inspired the writers/compilers of Scripture to include multiple statements by Jesus saying the same thing over and over: "Do not judge, and you will not be judged. Do not condemn, and you will not be condemned. Forgive, and you will be forgiven" (Luke 6:37). "Whenever you stand praying, forgive, if you have anything against anyone, so that your Father who is in heaven will also forgive you your transgressions" (Mark 11:25). *Wow! Forgive me to the same degree, in the same way, to the same extent, that I forgive others!* I better not hold a grudge. I better not store up bitterness. I better not keep a long list of wrongs suffered if I expect God to forgive me…. This is pretty radical, and very liberating.

Jesus finishes teaching his example of prayer by saying "Lead us not into temptation, but deliver us from the evil one (Guide and protect me, God, because you know, better than I do, what's best for me.)" That's the example that Jesus taught. In English, it's just 52 words. Not long at all! Augustine wrote "It was your Lord who put an end to long-windedness, so that you would not pray as if you wanted to teach God by your many words. Piety, not verbosity, is in order when you pray, since he knows all your needs." What better way to begin each day than using the model of prayer that Jesus personally taught his inquiring disciples to pray!

Well, it's fair to ask "Why pray at all? If God loves us and knows all we need before we pray, then why pray?" George MacDonald answers, "What if God knows *prayer* to be the thing we need first and most? What if the main object in God's idea of prayer be the supplying of our great, our endless need—the need of *himself*? What if the good of all our smaller and lower needs lies in this; that they help drive us to God? Communion with God is the one need of the soul beyond all other needs; prayer is the beginning of that communion."[21]

And finally, what prayer isn't: prayer isn't a magic formula—just pray and it happens, like a genie in a bottle. This reminds me of the story

---

[21] George MacDonald. *Unspoken Sermons* (1867-1889) (NYC: Cosimo Books), 166.

of an auto dealer, facing bankruptcy, was walking along a beach when he kicked a bottle and out popped a genie. "Thanks for setting me free," said the genie. "To show my appreciation, I'll grant you one wish." "Okay," said the auto dealer, "I want to be the only foreign car dealer in a major metropolitan market." "Done!" cried the genie. Immediately, the dealer found himself in a glass-walled office looking out over a major city. "Quick," he said to his secretary, "tell me who I am." "You're the only Cadillac dealer in downtown Tokyo," said the secretary. No, the power of prayer is not in the praying—"Well I prayed for it..." The power of prayer is in the One whom we pray to! Prayer is powerful, not because of the words we say, or even because of the fact that we prayed, but because of the good and gracious and generous and powerful God who hears and answers prayer.

In his book, *Too Busy Not to Pray*, Bill Hybels writes "God always answers prayer. If the *request* is wrong, God says, 'No.' If the *timing* is wrong, God says, 'Slow.' If *you* are wrong, God says, 'Grow.' But if the request is right, the timing is right, and you are right, God says, 'Go!'"[22] Prayer is a means of intimate communion, fellowship, and dependence upon God the Father who has promised to work in and through us through his Son, just as God worked through him. Prayer is a means of claiming God's promises and knowing and becoming abandoned to God's will.

5 lessons from the prayer life of Jesus

Let's look at the life of Jesus and see if we can learn some lessons about prayer[23]. In Luke 3:21, we find the opening story of the beginning of Jesus' public ministry: "When all the people were being baptized, Jesus was baptized too. *And as he was praying* (literally "to wish forward!"), heaven was opened and the Holy Spirit descended on him in bodily form

---

[22] Bill Hybels, *Too Busy Not to Pray*, (Downers Grove, IL:InterVarsity, 1998).

[23] This five-point outline on the "Prayer Life of Jesus" is from a series of four messages in 2002 by Dave Rickert at Camp Berea's (Hebron, NH: www.berea.org) annual men's retreat called "Man Camp." Dave is the teaching elder of *Bethany Bible Chapel,* Conway, South Carolina.

like a dove. And a voice came from heaven: "You are my Son, whom I love; with you I am well pleased." The first principle about prayer that we can learn from Jesus is, "Don't start anything without praying first." If you're like me, you get an idea or a task in front of you, and you want to jump right in, get it going, make it happen! But Jesus would not proceed with ministry without the Spirit's power and the Father's approval. The Puritan author, John Bunyan, wrote "You can do more than pray, *after* you've prayed, but you cannot do more than pray *until* you have prayed."

The first day I began serving on the staff at Good News Bible Chapel I spent the first few hours outside, walking in a big circle around the entire campus, praying. I think I began to wear a path in the grass behind the building! I had a Chapel Directory with me and as I walked around I prayed through it for each individual and each household. I prayed for each ministry and ministry team. I prayed for our elders and our deacons. I prayed for our impact on the community. And I prayed that I would see what God is doing, what God is blessing, and be part of that work of God.

Praying before you begin anything admits your dependence on God's power, and God's guidance, and God's blessing. Praying before you begin keeps you from thinking and acting like you're independent and self-sufficient. One guy put it this way: "Dear God, So far today I've done all right. I haven't gossiped, I haven't lost my temper, I haven't been greedy, grumpy, nasty, selfish or over-indulgent. I'm very thankful for that. But in a few minutes, God, I'm going to get out of bed, and from then on, I'm probably going to need a lot of help." So before you start the day, before you begin a project, before you sit in the meeting, before you start a new job or launch a new business, before you begin a new school year or a new game, before you take a trip—begin with prayer. That's what Jesus did.

The second principle of prayer that we can learn from Jesus is in Mark chapter 1, verse 35. It says "Very early in the morning, while it was still dark, Jesus got up, left the house and went off to a solitary place, where he prayed." This happened in the middle of an incredible period of activity for Jesus. Verse 21 says that "They (that is, Jesus and his disciples) went to Capernaum, and when the Sabbath came, Jesus went into the synagogue and began to teach. The people were amazed at his teaching, because he taught them as one who had authority, not as the teachers of the law." A few verses later, Jesus casts demons out of a demon possessed man. And the busy day continues. Verse 29 says "As soon as they left the synagogue, they went with James and John to the home of Simon and Andrew. Simon's mother-in-law was in bed with a fever, and they told Jesus about her. So he went to her, took her hand and helped her up. The fever left her and she began to wait on them." And it kept on coming. Look at verse 32: "That evening after sunset the people brought to Jesus all the sick and demon-possessed. The whole town gathered at the door, and Jesus healed many who had various diseases. He also drove out many demons..." What a day!

And now we come to verse 35: "Very early in the morning, while it was still dark, Jesus got up, left the house and went off to a solitary place, where he prayed." The second principle is: the busier he got, the more he prayed. In fact, Jesus' ministry activity was very busy and very successful and he still thought it was important to pray. When we are busy—successful or not—it is very tempting to get to work and not spend time praying. But Jesus knew that the power for living, the power for serving, the power for effective ministry comes from intimate connection with the Father, intimacy that is found in prayer. Martin Luther has been credited with saying, "I have so much business I cannot get on without spending three hours daily in prayer." If anything good, anything important, anything of lasting value is going to happen, it needs to be soaked in prayer. The busier Jesus got, the more he prayed.

The third principle on prayer that we can learn from Jesus is, "When we least feel like praying is when we need to pray the most." Look at Luke chapter 5, verse 15: "Yet the news about him spread all the more, so that crowds of people came to hear him and to be healed of their sicknesses. But Jesus *often* (did you catch that?) *often* withdrew to lonely places and prayed." I'm sure that he was physically and emotionally exhausted. I suspect he wanted sleep more than anything else. But he still made time to pray. When you are struggling with an issue—maybe circumstances are closing in, maybe you're struggling with your faith and doubts are filling your mind, maybe you're wrestling with a sinful habit—and actually, to be honest, you'd really rather give in! When you *least* feel like praying is when you need to pray the *most*. Don't put it off! Don't miss the opportunity to get strength and help and hope! Hebrews 4:14 says "Therefore, since we have a great high priest who has gone through the heavens, Jesus the Son of God, let us hold firmly to the faith we profess. For we do not have a high priest who is unable to sympathize with our weaknesses, but we have one who has been tempted in every way, just as we are—yet was without sin. Let us then approach the throne of grace with confidence, so that we may receive mercy and find grace to help us in our time of need." When we least feel like praying is when we need to pray the most.

The fourth principle says "Always pray before making important decisions." In Luke 6 we read the story of Jesus choosing who would be his students, his disciples: "One of those days Jesus went out to a mountainside to pray, and spent the night praying to God. When morning came, he called his disciples to him and chose twelve of them, whom he also designated apostles..." (Luke 6:12 & 13).

When you are facing an important decision, big or little—who to marry, where to go to school, which job to take—bathe that decision-making process in prayer. The more important the decision, the more that decision needs to be soaked in prayer. Jesus spent a whole night in prayer before selecting his disciples. Deb and I usually take a piece of paper, we make two columns, and make a list of the pros in one column and the cons in the other column—just to be sure we're being clear headed and we're taking all the details into account. That's the rational approach. But if the decision is going to be *blessed* by God, it must first be *brought* to God in prayer. I remember talking with my parents about decisions when I was a kid, and my mom would always ask "Did you pray about it?" Again, bringing all your decision to God in prayer acknowledges his Lordship, his authority, his sovereign rule in all things. Prayer acknowledges God's power and helps us to submit to his will and his plan and his timing. Praying before decisions helps to position your decision making in the big picture of *God's* priorities and eternal values. Proverbs 3:5, 6 is a good life verse for you to underline in your Bible, to memorize and remember: "Trust in the LORD with all your heart and lean not on your own understanding; in all your ways acknowledge him, and he will make your paths straight." Always pray before making important decisions.

Finally, prayer principle number five, "The habit of a lifetime of prayer can't be quenched in the hour of trial." In Dr. Luke's account of the crucifixion of Jesus he writes "It was now about the sixth hour, and darkness came over the whole land until the ninth hour, for the sun stopped shining. And the curtain of the temple was torn in two. Jesus called out with a loud voice, 'Father, into your hands I commit my spirit!' When he had said this, he breathed his last" (Luke 23:44-46). When the final moments came, Jesus—who began his ministry with prayer; who prayed the busier he got; who prayed, even when he might not have felt like it; who prayed before making important decisions—when the final moments came, after a lifetime of prayer, the habit of praying could not be quenched.

Don't wait until things are tough to begin to figure out how to pray—remember the hiker and the bear. Don't wait until you run out of alternatives to begin to pray. Don't go through a lifetime of prayerlessness and then on your deathbed, turn to prayer. When the trials of life, and death, are happening; when tough stuff is all around; the habit of a lifetime of prayer will make it easy for you to trust in God, to turn the circumstances over to God and say "Father, into your hands I commend my spirit."

Today is a good time to begin developing that habit of a lifetime of prayer. Decide now to begin each day with prayer. Decide now to pray, even when life is getting busier. Resolve now to pray, even when you don't feel like it. Choose now to bathe all your decisions in prayer. Begin a life of prayer now, a habit of prayer that will go the distance.

Digging deeper...

● If suddenly you were ordered like Daniel to never pray again (read his story in *Daniel,* chapter 6), what difference would that make in your life? Would you miss it? Write out your honest assessment on the place/priority prayer has in your life today.

● Which of the five lessons on prayer from the life of Jesus in this chapter rings deep with you? Why?

● Assignment: Some find it helpful to concentrate on prayer when they write out their prayers word for word while others like to keep a prayer journal and make notes on answers to prayer. What works best for you? Try a new "prayer tool" this week and watch what difference it makes.

CHAPTER 8

Command #5:

Love God...

"'Teacher, which is the greatest commandment in the Law?' Jesus replied: 'Love the Lord your God with all your heart and with all your soul and with all your mind. This is the first and greatest commandment. And the second is like it: Love your neighbor as yourself.'"
- Matthew 22:36-40

"What we are worshipping we are becoming."
- Ralph Waldo Emerson

"We resemble what we revere for our ruin or restoration."[24]
- G. K. Beale

God wants to be worshipped. That's the whole story of the Bible from Genesis to Revelation—God is raising up for himself worshipers from every language, tribe and nation. God wants us to know him. He's not hiding. God is not playing some sort of cosmic game of hide-and-seek, hiding behind a tree saying "You're getting warmer." God is not trying to cover himself up. He has worked really hard to reveal himself and he wants us to know him. He has revealed himself first in the complexity

---

[24] Gregory K. Beale, *We Become What We Worship: A theology of idolatry.* (Downers Grove: IVP Academic, 2008)

and beauty of his creation. The Psalm writer could say "The heavens declare the glory of God; the skies proclaim the work of his hands." (Psalm 19:1). And second, he has revealed himself to us clearly in his word, the Bible. And finally, he has revealed himself completely to us by sending us his one and only Son, Jesus. "In the past God spoke to our forefathers through the prophets at many times and in various ways, but in these last days he has spoken to us by his Son," (Hebrews 1:1,2). "No one has ever seen God; the only God, who is at the Father's side, he has made him known." (John 1:18 ESV). It seems like God is going to pretty extreme lengths to be known. And while we don't understand all that God is, we can grasp some things about him in what he has revealed.

We Worship God For Who He Is...
In Matthew 22:36-40, Jesus' is quoting from Deuteronomy 6:4-5, calling on us to forsake anything that takes God's place and worship him with all of our being—heart, soul and mind. God's radical total separateness, his transcendent *"wholly otherness"*[25] is the basis for our worship. *"There is no god like you, O Lord!"* Let's look first at a few specific attributes of God that make me want to worship him. And then I want to talk with you about loving the Lord with all your heart.

First and foremost, we need to grasp what it means when the Bible tells us that God is holy. To be holy is to be separate, set apart. And in the case of God, we say that God is holy, set apart from anything impure, anything unclean, anything ... "ungodly!" In fact, I think that holiness is the key defining character attribute of God. Turn in your bible with me for a moment to Isaiah, in the middle of the Old Testament, the book by the prophet Isaiah, chapter 6. This is the story of how Isaiah got his assignment from God to be a prophet. I mean, how do you get to be a prophet? Do you just wake up one morning and decide on a career change? *I used to be a goat herder but now I want to be a prophet?*

Isaiah chapter 6, let's read from verse 1:

---

[25] Barth, Karl. *The Humanity of God*, trans. John Newton Thomas and Thomas Wieser. (Atlanta: John Knox Press, 1960), 37.

> In the year that King Uzziah died, I (this is Isaiah talking here) I saw the Lord seated on a throne (some sort of supernatural vision experience) I saw the Lord seated on a throne, high and exalted, and the train of his robe filled the temple. Above him were seraphs, each with six wings: With two wings they covered their faces, with two they covered their feet, and with two they were flying. And they were calling to one another: "Holy, holy, holy is the LORD Almighty; the whole earth is full of his glory." (Underline that verse in your bible) At the sound of their voices the doorposts and thresholds shook and the temple was filled with smoke. "Woe to me!" I cried. "I am ruined! For I am a man of unclean lips, and I live among a people of unclean lips, and my eyes have seen the King, the LORD Almighty. Then one of the seraphs flew to me with a live coal in his hand, which he had taken with tongs from the altar. With it he touched my mouth and said, "See, this has touched your lips; your guilt is taken away and your sin atoned for."

Bob Deffinbaugh writes that "The death of King Uzziah seems to have spelled the end of an era, a golden era, for the southern Kingdom of Judah. The "good times" were over; the "hard times" were about to commence as verses 9 and 10 indicate. Isaiah's ministry is opening from a human point of view at the very worst possible time. His ministry was not going to be regarded a success (as if many of the prophets of old were "successful,' with the singular exception of Jonah!). Isaiah was in for a chilly reception. He and his message would be spurned. What did Isaiah need to give him the proper perspective and endurance to persevere in such hard times? The answer: a vision of God himself!"[26]

This is precisely what God gave to Isaiah—a dramatic revelation of himself in all his holiness. Isaiah saw the Lord sitting enthroned in heaven, lofty and exalted. The angels who stood above him were magnificent, and they called out to one another, "Holy, Holy, Holy, is the

---

[26] Deffinbaugh, Bob. http://bible.org/seriespage/holiness-god; accessed 6/13/2010.

LORD of hosts, the whole earth is full of His glory" (verse 3). The earth was rocked with earthquakes at this declaration and the temple was filled with smoke. It was as dramatic and powerful a vision of God and his holiness as one could every possibly wish to see.

Deffinbaugh notes that Isaiah's response to this personal stage pass audience with God is far from what we hear today from many who claim special experiences with God. Isaiah came away not impressed with his "importance." His "self-esteem" was not enhanced. Actually, just the opposite took place. His vision of the holiness of God caused Isaiah to lament his own utter sinfulness. If God was holy, Isaiah clearly saw that he was not. Isaiah confessed his own un-holiness and that of his people.

If Isaiah was going to be the spokesman for God during tough times, was going to be rejected and persecuted, he had to know that God was not "just like him, only better." No, God is totally different; God is holy, we're not.

So notice back in Isaiah 6, verse 3, what those angels were calling out to each other. They cried "Holy, holy, holy, is the Lord God Almighty! The whole earth is filled with his glory!" Holy, holy, holy. R.C. Sproul writes "The Bible says that God is holy, holy, holy. Not that He is merely holy, or even holy, holy. He is holy, holy, holy!"[27] Three times holy!

Turn in your bible to Revelation, the last book of the bible, the Revelation of Jesus Christ as recorded by the apostle John, Revelation, chapter 4. And let's get a second report of what the throne room of heaven is like. Revelation, chapter four, look down at verse two:

> At once I was in the Spirit (this is the apostle John telling us about his supernatural vision)... At once I was in the Spirit, and there before me was a throne in heaven with someone sitting on it. And the one who sat there had the appearance of jasper and carnelian (fine, deep colored gemstones). A rainbow, resembling an emerald, encircled the throne. Surrounding the throne were twenty-four other thrones, and seated on them were twenty-four elders. They were dressed

---

[27] R. C. Sproul. *The Holiness of God* (Carol Stream, IL: Tyndale House, 2nd edition, 2000), 26.

in white and had crowns of gold on their heads. From the throne came flashes of lightning, rumblings and peals of thunder. Before the throne, seven lamps were blazing. These are the seven spirits of God. Also before the throne there was what looked like a sea of glass, clear as crystal.

In the center, around the throne, were four living creatures, and they were covered with eyes, in front and in back. The first living creature was like a lion, the second was like an ox, the third had a face like a man, the fourth was like a flying eagle (very symbolic language). Each of the four living creatures had six wings and was covered with eyes all around, even under his wings. Day and night they never stop saying: "*Holy, holy, holy* is the Lord God Almighty, who was, and is, and is to come." (Revelation 4:2-8).[28]

Two visions of the throne room of heaven; both hear the cry "Holy, holy, holy, is the Lord God almighty!" I think that helps confirm for us that in heaven, those closest to the throne of God recognize his holiness as his foremost attribute. The primary meaning of *holy* is 'separate.' It comes from an ancient word that meant, 'to cut,' or 'to separate.' The late Lewis Smedes, a seminary professor of theology and ethics and an author best known for his book called *Forgive and Forget*, tells of the time he was trimming some lettuce on a cutting board in the kitchen and in an instant his sharp knife sliced off the very thin tip of one finger. He says that he stood there for a moment, just looking at the tip of his finger lying there, cut off, separate, by itself, on the cutting board. And, theologian that he was, he thought, "That's holy! Cut off! Separate!"

Perhaps even more accurate would be the phrase "a cut above something." When we find a garment or another piece of merchandise that is outstanding, that has a superior excellence, we use the expression that it is "a cut above the rest."

---

[28] Underline verse eight in your Bible and out in the margin write "Is 6:3;" in Isaiah 6:3, write in the margin, "Rev 4:8" to connect those two verses together.

This means that the one who is holy is uniquely holy, with no rivals, no competition, no one to even be compared to. Again R.C. Sproul writes "When the Bible calls God *holy* it means primarily that God is transcendentally separate. He is so far above and beyond us that He seems almost totally foreign to us. To be holy is to be 'other,' to be different in a special way."[29] The Scriptures put it this way: Exodus 15:11: "Who among the gods is like you, O LORD? Who is like you, majestic in holiness, Awesome in glory, working wonders?" 1 Samuel 2:2: "There is no one holy like the LORD, Indeed, there is no one besides you, there is no rock like our God."

> *Psalm 86:8-10* - Among the gods there is none like you, O Lord; no deeds can compare with yours. All the nations you have made will come and worship before you, O Lord; they will bring glory to your name. For you are great and do marvelous deeds; you alone are God.

So first, to be holy is to be separate, "wholly other," greater than, transcendent. Second, God is holy in every aspect of His nature and character. R.C. Sproul continues "We often describe God by compiling a list of qualities or characteristics that we call his *attributes*. We say that God is a spirit, that he knows everything, that he is loving, just, merciful, gracious, eternal, all-powerful, and so on. The tendency is to add the idea of being holy to this long list of attributes as one more attribute among many. But when the word *holy* is applied to God, it does not signify one single attribute. On the contrary, God is called holy in a general sense. The word is used as a synonym for his deity. That is, the word *holy* calls attention to *all* that God is. It reminds us that his love is holy love, his justice is holy justice, his mercy is holy mercy, his knowledge is holy knowledge..."[30] Did you notice from our texts in Isaiah 6 and Revelation 4 that the Bible never says that God is love, love, love. (Yes, John tells us repeatedly that the essence of God is love. God is

---

[29] Sproul, R. C. *The Holiness of God* , 38.
[30] *Ibid.* 39, 40

characterized as love. Do you want to know love? Get to know God.) But when these angels around God in the courts of heaven fly around the throne of God Almighty they don't cry out "Love, love, love is the Lord God almighty!" There are some people today, some scholars,[31] even some pretty cool and popular preachers—and more than a few book writers—who want us to think that God's love trumps all. So much so that they claim God could never judge or punish sin, because he's ... *love!*

But the Bible never says that God is love, love, love or mercy, mercy, mercy, or even wrath, wrath, wrath, or justice, justice, justice. It *does* say that He is *holy, holy, holy,* the whole earth is full of His glory." Pastor and author Tony Evans says this about God: "Holiness is the centerpiece of God's attributes. Of all the things God is, at the center of His being, God is holy. Never in the Bible is God called, 'love, love, love,' or 'eternal, eternal, eternal,' or 'truth, truth, truth.' he is never emphatically called by any other name except one: "Holy, Holy, Holy is the lord of Hosts!" (Isaiah 6:3).[32]

So first, to be holy is to be separate, "wholly other," greater than, transcendent. Second, God is holy in every aspect of His nature and character. Third, to be holy is to be *morally pure*. When things are made holy, when they are consecrated, they are set apart for a special purpose and not to be used for anything else but that special purpose, like our cutting board.

---

[31] In his contribution to *Global God: Multicultural Evangelical Views of God* (Spencer & Spencer, Baker, 1998), Dr. William David Spencer, writing in the second chapter from Exodus 34:6, notes "...love is God's primary attribute," and again "The good news of Christianity is that God's primary love took precedence among God's attributes ..." (p. 42). This unbalanced emphasis is most likely willing blindness influenced by contemporary social constructs.

The logical extension of this well-intentioned but misguided emotionalism bears its fruit in Rob Bell's *Love Wins: A Book About Heaven, Hell and the Fate of Every Person Who Ever Lived* (Harper One, 2011) where he argues from the primacy of God's love for what all except Bell recognize as universalism (the idea that everyone will eventually be saved because God to "too loving" to condemn anyone to hell). Bell writes "At the center of the Christian tradition since the first church have been a number who insist that history is not tragic, hell is not forever, and love, in the end, wins and all will be reconciled to God" (p. 109). In choosing the title of his book from this sentence, Bell embraces the idea.

[32] Evans, Tony. *Our God is Awesome* (Chicago: Moody Press, 1994), 79.

Habakkuk 1:13 says "Your eyes O Lord, are too pure to look on evil; you cannot tolerate wrong." Psalm 24:3, 4: "Who may ascend into the hill of the LORD? And who may stand in His holy place? He who has clean hands and a pure heart, who has not lifted up his soul to falsehood, and has not sworn deceitfully." If you're going to stand in the presence of holy, holy, holy God, you sure better be pure.

Now there's a problem here. You may be better than the guy sitting next to you. And I know some things about myself that you don't know so I'm pretty *sure* that you're better than me. But I'm also pretty sure that you're no "Mother Teresa." I'm pretty sure that an honest assessment would reveal that you're not remotely up to God's standard of purity. I guess that means that you're just like me.

I was reading in Psalm 103 a while back for my daily devos: "...for God knows how we are formed, he remembers that we are dust." He knows all about you and me and knows how fragile and imperfect and broken we are. The bible calls that brokenness sin. Romans 3:23 says "All have sinned and fall short of God's perfect standard." Even Mother Teresa.[33] And that's where Jesus comes into the picture.

The story of the bible, from cover to cover, is the story of God greatly wanting a relationship with his creation, he wants them to worship him and praise him, and enjoy him forever. But they mess up and get all independent and mess up the perfect garden of delight by disobedience.

So then God makes a special relationship with one particular family and promises that he will bless them and make them like the sand on the seashore and the stars in the sky; he'll be their God and they'll be his people. And they still mess up and get all independent and rebellious and actually prostitute themselves with fake god-wanna-bes.

So finally God sends his one and only, perfect Son, Jesus, who comes to earth. What's that? That's the transcendent ... becoming immanent; that which was far off, coming very near; the unknowable, becoming

---

[33] And while Mother Teresa herself was surely a much better person than I, she still desperately needed a savior. Isaiah 59:2 tells us "Your iniquities have separated you from your God; your sins have hidden his face from you, so that he will not hear."

knowable; the incomprehensible, finally being revealed. If you want to know God, get to know Jesus.

Jesus leaves heaven, takes on a body just like his own creation, dies a horrible death on the cross in the place of his creatures so that they can finally be forgiven, washed clean, made pure and can finally stand before God. 1 Peter 3:18 says "For Christ died for sins once for all, the righteous for the unrighteous, to bring you to God," literally, take that which is unclean and make it fit to come right into the very presence of the Holy One.

Remember the last few verses that we read in Isaiah 6: "Then one of the seraphs flew to me with a live coal in his hand, which he had taken with tongs from the altar. With it he touched my mouth and said, 'See, this has touched your lips; your guilt is taken away and your sin atoned for.'" God, in his mercy and love, provided a way for the unholy to be made holy, the unclean to be made clean. Because of the work of Jesus on the cross in your place and mine, you and I can stand in the presence of a holy, holy, holy God.

This isn't just a theology lesson. This is a *declaration of freedom* from the burden of the guilt of your sin! *Your* guilt is taken away and *your* sin atoned for. And in God's eyes, he now sees all who believe in Jesus as the forgiver of their sin and the leader of their life as sinless, spotless, dressed up in the neat, clean clothes of Jesus. 2 Corinthians 5:21 tells us that "God made him (that's Jesus) God made Jesus who had no sin to *be* sin for us, so that in him we might become the righteousness of God!"

The tiny book by the prophet Hosea is at the back of the Old Testament half of your Bible. In chapter 6, verse 6, God says to the prophet Hosea "For I desire mercy, not sacrifice, and acknowledgment of God rather than burnt offerings." God is more concerned that you *know him* and *acknowledge him* than he is that you do some sort of regular religious ritual. He is not a God of our own wishes. Nor a God of our own design. Too much of contemporary Christianity has reduced the holy, holy, holy God to our own level—just like us, only a bit better.

Granted, it's not easy knowing God. After all, a God that I can completely know and understand wouldn't be much of a God at all. "As the heavens are higher than the earth, so are my ways higher than your ways and my thoughts than your thoughts" says the Lord (Isaiah 55:9). He is beyond understanding. But fortunately, he has revealed some things for us to wrestle with, to meditate on.

For example, the Bible tells us that God is immutable—that is, he is unchanging, always the same. Listen to Malachi 3:6: "I the LORD do not change..." In James 1:17 James, the half-brother of Jesus, wrote "Every good and perfect gift is from above, coming down from the Father of the heavenly lights, *who does not change like shifting shadows.*" God never changes. God can never get better. God can never become somehow weaker or worse. There is nothing about him that can or will ever change. When we say that he will never change we mean that his character will never change. God will always, in every circumstance, be a holy God of love and mercy and justice. And his will and plan never changes. Numbers 23:19 says "God is not a man, that he should lie, Nor a son of man, that he should change his mind; does he speak and then not act? Does he promise and not fulfill?" God may choose to react differently to the responses of mankind. He told Jonah to go to Nineveh and tell them that their city would be destroyed because of their sin. Jonah went, reluctantly, the people heard his message and turned from their sin and repented. The text tells us that God didn't bring the destruction that he had promised. Had God changed? No, *the people had changed.* And God acted as he always acts toward those who repent. God is immutable, unchanging; he always acts consistently to his character and his will.

The truth of God's immutability is great comfort for us. It means that his love for you *never changes.* As Philip Yancy wrote in *What's So Amazing About Grace,* "There's nothing that we can do to make God love us more. .... And there's nothing that we can do to make God love us less."[34] God's love for you is unchanging! God's grace to you in Jesus Christ is unchanging! God's promises to you are unchanging!

---

[34] Philip Yancy, *What's So Amazing About Grace.* (Grand Rapids: Zondervan, 1997), 70.

God is immutable, unchanging in his character and will and, second, God is omnipotent—all powerful; there is nothing that God cannot do. Isaiah 14:24 - "The LORD Almighty has sworn, 'Surely, as I have planned, *so it will be*,[35] and as I have purposed, *so it will stand*. (Jump down to verse 26) This is the plan determined for the whole world; this is the hand stretched out over all nations. For the LORD Almighty has purposed, and who can thwart him? His hand is stretched out, and who can turn it back?'" Underline those verses in your Bible in Isaiah 14: 24, 26 and 27. Write "God's purpose will stand!" in the margin. Now look ahead a few pages to Isaiah, chapter 46, verse 9: "Remember the former things, those of long ago; I am God, and there is no other; I am God, and there is none like me. I make known the end from the beginning, from ancient times, what is still to come. I say: 'My purpose will stand, and I will do *all* that I please. From the east I summon a bird of prey; from a far-off land, a man to fulfill my purpose. What I have said, that will I bring about; what I have planned, that will I do!'" Underline those verses in your Bible. And again in the margin write "God's purpose will stand!"

God is at work accomplishing his plan. Nothing can stop him. Let's look quickly at three areas where we can see God's omnipotence, his irresistible power at work. First, God's power can be seen in making something from nothing. Psalms 33:6 tells us "By the word of the LORD were the heavens made, their starry host by the breath of his mouth." Scientists work very hard to understand what happened in the moments of creation. They admit that there was a beginning; that there was a moment in time when the universe did not exist, and then suddenly it existed. Right now, thousands of the world's best scientists are hoping that CERN's 20 kilometer Hadron Collider, buried 100 meters beneath the farmlands of Switzerland and France, will explain what happened in the nanoseconds *after* the beginning of the universe. The ALICE experiment uses the Large Hadron Collider to recreate conditions similar to those pico-seconds after creation, in particular to analyze the properties of the quark-gluon plasma. But as much as they know, none

---

[35] My italics in this verse.

will say just how or exactly where our universe came from; what was the *first cause*. The Bible tells us that God is the great creator who made something from nothing.

Second, God sustains creation. Hebrews 1:3 tells us that "The Son is the radiance of God's glory and the exact representation of his being, sustaining all things by his powerful word." God rested from the work of creating on the seventh day. But he is still sustaining all he has created.

Third, God can redeem the lost. 1 Corinthians 1 tells us: "Brothers, think of what you were when you were called. Not many of you were wise by human standards; not many were influential; not many were of noble birth. But God chose the foolish things of the world to shame the wise; God chose the weak things of the world to shame the strong. He chose the lowly things of this world and the despised things—and the things that are not—to nullify the things that are, so that no one may boast before him. (Verse 30) It is because of him that you are in Christ Jesus, who has become for us wisdom from God—that is, our righteousness, holiness and redemption. Therefore, as it is written: 'Let him who boasts boast in the Lord!'"

God's omnipotence, his irresistible power, brings me to worship. Psalm 121 says "I lift up my eyes to the hills—where does my help come from? My help comes from the LORD, the Maker of heaven and earth." Psalm 20:7 says "Some trust in chariots and some in horses, but we trust in the name of the LORD our God." When I'm afraid I'm reminded that Proverbs 18:10 says "The name of the LORD is a strong tower; the righteous run to it and are safe." When I'm anxious I remember 1 John 4:4: "Greater is he that is in me than he who is in the world." When I lack confidence I remember Phil 4:13 "I can do all things through Christ who strengthens me!" A clear vision of the unchanging, all-powerful, holy, holy, holy God brings a sense of stability and security in our very unstable and insecure lives and moves us to worship....

Now that we've taken a look at who God is and why we should love him, let's discuss what living him actually looks like. In Isaiah 29:13 The Lord says "These people come near to me with their mouth and honor me with their lips, but their hearts are far from me. Their worship of me is made up only of rules taught by men." It's pretty easy to come up with a prescription for worship. I've actually had some folks say "The people here don't know how to worship. They won't (now you fill in the blank depending on the conversation) a. raise their hands, or b. clap their hands, or c. sing out loud, or d. shout "Hallelujah!" The list goes on. These folks are sincere and mean well, and I do not want to discourage them or demean their own worship. I'm actually very glad that they have a clear picture in their mind and their own experience about what it means *for them* to worship God.

But what God *doesn't* need is worship that is "made up only of rules taught by men." No, we should never say "This is how you must worship, like this..." Because God is much more interested in what your heart is saying than where your hands are parked. God is more concerned for your heart's passion than your posture. God is listening more for the quiet murmurs of your heart than he is for the volume level of your voice. And the authentic expressions of your heart in worship might look quite different than mine. Let's take Abraham for example. You remember, Abraham had heard God's voice tell him to leave his homeland and go to a distant and strange land (look again at Genesis 12). Abraham obeyed God and received a great promise from God. And it seems that everywhere that Abraham went, he built altars to God and offered sacrifices. But we don't have a record of any songs that he wrote. And we don't have any record of him dancing before God. Abraham built altars and offered sacrifices.

Then we have the apostle Paul. We don't have any record of Paul building altars. But he thought deeply about and wrote about the incredible mysteries of God's love and grace for lost and broken people. He wrote out for us the profound truths of redemption by the blood of Jesus on the cross, and justification by faith, and what it means to be far off from God because of sin and then adopted into the family of God by his grace shown in Jesus on the cross. And frequently, at the end of his heavy and deep theological thoughts, Paul breaks into short, spontaneous prayers of praise to God. So in Romans 11 he can't take it any more and breaks out with "Oh, the depth of the riches of the wisdom and knowledge of God! How unsearchable his judgments, and his paths beyond tracing out! Who has known the mind of the Lord? Or who has been his counselor? Who has ever given to God, that God should repay him? For from him and through him and to him are all things. To him be the glory forever! Amen!"

Then we have Moses and Elijah, confronting power and evil and standing up for justice for the oppressed. There's John, with his powerful, stunning, sensuous visions of the awesome power and wrath and glory of God in heaven.

And then there's David, "a man after God's own heart." David wrote dozens of poems of praise and many of our praise songs that we sing on Sunday mornings. He also wrote very intimate and personal reflections on God's mercy and love that came out of his own deep emotions. And of course David is also the one who danced with joy before the Lord and crowds of people—he danced with such carefree abandon that he humiliated himself and embarrassed his wife.

There's David's conflicted son, Solomon, who built a magnificent temple to God and offered extravagant sacrifices even though he was compromised in his relationships. And there's the woman who poured out an expensive gift on Jesus' feet and wiped his feet with her tears. And then there's Mary, the sister of Martha and Lazarus, who was quite content to just sit quietly at Jesus' feet in the posture of a learning disciple, just to be with him and listen to him and not say or do anything at all.

Each was very different. Some public. Some private. Some loud. Some quiet. Some that seemed to us to be quite liturgical or ritualistic. Some that were very unique and individualistic. All different. No one model or prescription for us. All worshipping the same God. All with acceptable worship that pleased God and brought pleasure to God.

What did they all have in common? What did they all share that made their *very different worship* pleasing and acceptable to God? *A heart of love.* A heart that overflowed with love and gratitude. A heart that spilled over with joy and thanksgiving. A heart that was so full of personal enjoyment of God, so taken with his great love and mercy, so surrounded by his grace in their lives that they couldn't be quiet, couldn't stay away, couldn't restrain, couldn't hold back the worship.

And how did their heart get that way? What brought them to that place of worship? What happened that prepared their heart before the time of worship? Time alone with God. Time spent talking to God. Time spent in his presence in prayer. Time spent quietly thinking or writing about his great goodness, his awesome deeds. Time deliberately recalling and rehearsing what God had done in their lives. Time spent listening to God reveal himself to them through Scripture, through observing his creation, through studying the deep truths of doctrine, through the marvel in the stunning complexity of a newborn baby or the glory of a golden sunset, and most of all, through his Son Jesus.

You may not be David or Mary. You might not be John or Paul or Abraham or the woman with the alabaster jar of precious perfume. But you can spend time alone with God and remember his mercy and love for *you*; recall and rehearse his acts of redemption and healing in *your* life. And you can let thoughts of his love and grace and mercy so fill *your* heart that they flow over into praise and worship. And you can meet together with other Christ-followers on Sundays, not to "get moved to worship," but to pour out from the overflow of your heart of what has already been happening in worship on Monday and Tuesday and Wednesday and Thursday and Friday and Saturday. And he'll be very pleased with that, no matter where you are, no matter what it looks and sounds like.

Digging deeper...

- Loving God is grounded in knowing God. Read Isaiah 6:1-5 then write down your thoughts on what it means that God is "Wholly other."

- What about God's creation strikes you as amazing and wonderful and beyond cool? Write down a few thoughts and take a few minutes to praise and worship God in prayer or a song about that...

● Life for many of us is crazy busy and very loud. What structures can you put in your life—weekly, monthly, annually—to give you some time for worship? For silence and solitude alone with God? What would that look like?

Worshipping God with...	... my Time	... my Talent	...my Treasure
Weekly			
Monthly			
Annually			

Pray that you would begin to act on this plan, reshaping the time and priorities of your life for actively seeking God in quietness, in solitude, in prayer.

CHAPTER 9

...love one another...

"A new command I give you: Love one another.
As I have loved you, so you must love one another.
By this all men will know that you are my disciples,
if you love one another."
- John 13:34, 35

The late Francis Schaeffer wrote a thin book that changed my life. I remember it well. It was the hot summer of 1970 and I was working as the Waterfront Director at Camp Berea, a Christian summer camp on Newfound Lake at the edge of the White Mountains in New Hampshire. The tiny, one-room bookstore at Berea had one or two copies of a few dozen books. This one was small and inexpensive, only 38 pages! Just right for a high school kid. It was short but it was powerful. So when I read *The Mark of the Christian* that summer, it changed everything.

Schaeffer opened with "Christians have not always presented a pretty picture to the world. Too often they have failed to show the beauty of love, the beauty of Christ, the holiness of God. And the world has turned away."[36] With those words he began a passionate argument aimed at followers of Jesus for taking his command to love each other both literally and seriously. Noting that all disciples of Jesus are to love God first and love our neighbor (and even our enemies), he then wrote that this particular command of Jesus in John 13:34, 35 is a *new*

---
[36] Francis A. Schaeffer *The Mark of the Christian* (Downers Grove, IL: InterVarsity Press, 1970), 5.

command precisely because it is "a command to have a special love to all true Christians, all born-again Christians." Pointing out that this command has "two cutting edges," Schaeffer explained that "it means we must distinguish true Christians from all pretenders and be sure that we leave no true Christians outside of our consideration." The challenge is clear: how do you identify the true Christians who are to be loved while avoiding both a circle that is too large and one that is too small?

And while we wrestle with this question, the plain words of Jesus in John 17:20, 21 add another layer of challenge: the world around us is going to judge whether Jesus has been sent by the Father on the basis of something that can be seen and measured—our love for one another.

> "My prayer is not for them alone. I pray also for those who will believe in me through their message, that all of them may be one, Father, just as you are in me and I am in you. May they also be in us so that the world may believe that you have sent me."

Let's take a few moments to look at these two challenges: first, drawing the right circle of "Christians" to love, and second, performing in front of the watching world. It is pretty obvious that not all who call themselves Christians are in fact born-again followers of Jesus. Now before you think I'm an arrogant jerk (which I may be, but hold your thoughts for a moment), I need to explain that I think there will be some in heaven who will surprise all of us—"How did he/she get here?" And the answer of course will be, "He/she got here the same way *anyone* does, by abandoning all hope of saving themselves and throwing all their trust and hope at the foot of the cross where Jesus died in their place so they can be forgiven, redeemed and restored to wholeness and new life." So if someone is in heaven that you or I can't imagine being there, it's only by the grace of God revealed in Jesus Christ.

Then again I suspect there might be quite a few who are *not* in heaven that we might have expected to be there. After all, they told us that they were Christians. They even showed up in church, carried a big Bible, maybe sang in the choir or taught Sunday School. So where are they? And I think then of the words of Jesus, "Later the others also came. 'Sir! Sir!' they said. 'Open the door for us!' But he replied, 'I tell you the truth, I don't know you'" (Matthew 25:11, 12). The bottom line is that ultimately God, and God alone, will decide in his great holiness, justice and grace who will be there, and who will not be (Revelation 20:11-15).

Now here's the thing; we are commanded to love them as a dear brother or sister in Christ, and if we are convinced by their fruit[37] that they are not an authentic follower of Jesus then we are commanded to ... love them anyway since we are to love our neighbor and even our enemy! There is no end run around the command to love those around us—love God, love each other, love your neighbor, love your enemy! Love the saved. Love the lost. Love them all!

But the sad history of the Christian church from Pentecost to today is that Christians are frequently divided, at odds with one another, and sometimes even in a nasty war of words and un-loving exclusions. It is true that Christ-followers cannot be linked as spiritual sisters and brothers with those who openly deny the orthodox biblical faith in the Trinity, who deny the final authority of the Word of God—the utopian desire to sit around the campfire together holding hands and sing "Kumbya my Lord" as if truth does not matter is just sappy, sentimental silliness. And spiritually dangerous. But on this side of that firm line of truth there is a wide circle of brothers and sisters in Christ which includes many who are unfamiliar to us. Maybe they worship God quite differently than we do. Maybe they use language that is unfamiliar or even uncomfortable to us. For myself, the final test is, "Will they be in

---

[37] Jesus said "You will know them by their fruit" (Matthew 7:16). Notice that the test is not their knowledge; not how much doctrine they know or how much of the bible they can explain. And the test is not one of association; what denomination, church or tradition they belong to. But rather Jesus said that the test is the fruit that is displayed in their life. Sadly, many who deny Jesus outright display finer fruit of love, joy, peace, patience, kindness, goodness, faithfulness, gentleness and self-control (the "Fruits of the Sprit" we find in Galatians 5:22, 23) than do many who openly confess Jesus as Lord.

heaven, falling on their face, worshipping God next to me for eternity?"[38] And when I consider the answer to that question I realize that the circle is indeed quite wide. So there surely will be some in heaven who used to worship at that church just down the street, one I drove by to go to my services on Sunday, the one with services that made me squirm a bit because they were so different. They talked a lot about things that I didn't see as that important in the Bible and I think they misunderstood some really important stuff; they even prayed very differently than I do. But are they saved by God's grace? I am quite sure than many of them are, and maybe many more than I imagine.

So if they are saved by God's grace and they'll be in heaven worshipping him for all eternity, then what does that mean for our relationship now? What about all the divisions we have now? The denominations? The separations? How should we understand that? What can we do about that? In a detailed and very insightful book, *One Lord, One Faith*, Rex Koivisto argues that there is really only one church in every community and it is the single universal mystical body of Christ made up of *every believer in that community* who is saved by God's amazing grace[39]—everyone who is simply believing with saving faith that Jesus alone is Lord and Savior—no matter what the name might be on the sign in front of the building they worship in. So for example, "the

---

[38] My "test"—"Will they be in heaven?"—is surely too simplistic on many levels. The late Donald Bloesch wrote "The key to ... unity lies in a common commitment to Jesus Christ as the divine Savior from sin, a common purpose to fulfill the Great Commission and a common acknowledgement of the absolute normativeness of Holy Scripture," *The Future of Evangelical Christianity: A call for unity amid diversity* (Downers Grove: InterVarsity Press, 1988), 6.

Rex Koivisto sees a simple concise "core orthodoxy" statement of the Gospel message as the unifying factor and suggests "simply this: God sent His Son into the world to die as an atonement for sin, and God raised Him from the dead, so that anyone who places faith in Him receives the free gift of salvation." *One Lord, One Faith: A theology for cross-denominational renewal* (Eugene, OR: Wipf & Stock, 2009), 232.

[39] "It becomes very apparent, then, that there were at root at least two 'levels' of the 'local church' in the New Testament era: the general area or 'city church' (which gathered infrequently) as well as the particular or 'house church' (which gathered frequently). ... The developed house church of the first century is thus to be understood as the equivalent of what is typically called the local church today. *Filmore Street Baptist* is one house church in a city; *Metro Presbyterian* is another; *Our Savior Lutheran* would be a third. The 'local church' in the city, on this understanding, would include them all, as well as other gatherings of believers in the apostolic Gospel of Christ at various locations in the city." Koivisto, *One Lord, One Faith*, 9, 11.

church of Attleboro" is all those followers of Jesus in my city of Attleboro, Massachusetts—not unlike the ancient church of Corinth or the fine church of Ephesus—no matter what their denomination, movement, affiliation, network or lack thereof, might be. The pastors/elders of those churches are in effect "the elders of the church of Attleboro." And like the early church of Jerusalem (with over 3,000 souls on the first day it was planted) which met in various homes (Acts 2:46; see also Rom 16:5, 1 Cor 16:9, Col 4:15, Phil 1:2) and yet was addressed as one church, in the same way "the church of Attleboro" meets in many locations yet is also only one church or "assembly of the called-out-ones."

The problem Koivisto says is the separatist sectarianism that results from loyalties to denominations and associations, traditions, networks and movements[40] that are stronger than the bond of love that unites all true followers of Jesus together. Koivisto notes that too often "loyalties are more to congregations of similar denominations *outside* the city than they are to different denominations *within* the city."[41] Rather than choose to ignore or even compete against the church down the street, Koivisto urges a change in attitude that recognizes and values the unity of the single body/bride of Christ in the city/town/village.[42] This means learning to recognize the common core in orthodox faith, "One Lord, one faith," and also learning to identify, appreciate and value the positive distinctives that the different traditions offer—which of course means we must be able to see the difference between that core orthodoxy and our chosen and beloved traditions. And begin to understand and accept that the benefit to be gained by all involved is "cooperation in

---

[40] For example, some within the Plymouth Brethren movement—the assembly heritage which I grew up in and am still associated with—are quick and proud to claim that they are not a denomination while yet ignoring the sad reality that pride in their traditions and distinctives disguised as "The correct understanding of the Bible" too often effectively separates them from brothers and sisters who otherwise are orthodox in faith and *Sola Scriptura*.

[41] Koivisto. *One Lord, One Faith*, 120.

[42] Koivisto, academic dean of the college and graduate school at Multnomah University in Portland, Oregon, puts it plainly: "If I understand that I am more closely related locally to other denominationally identified Christians in a local area than I am with denominationally similar Christians at a distant locality, working for unity in mission around a core orthodoxy becomes quite practical and real." *One Lord, One Faith*, 12, footnote 18.

evangelism and mission, cooperation in discipline, mutual prayer support, healthy theological dialogue and organizational coordination."[43]

Surely there will always be differences, distinctives and even disagreements between us; we will never agree on everything this side of glory. And I suspect we will all be surprised in glory to discover the real truth about some of those things we thought we understood so clearly and fought so hard for. But the day of denominational exclusivism is fading quickly. And fading none too soon as there will surely not be separated sections for Baptists, Wesleyans, Lutherans, Brethren and the 38,000 or so other Christian denominational groups in heaven. Fortunately the unity inherent in the bride and body of Christ does not necessarily require that we agree on every little detail. But we are instructed to "Submit to one another out of reverence for Christ" (Eph 5:21), "...in humility consider others better than yourselves" (Phil2:3), and to "look not only to your interests, but also to the interests of others" (Phil 2:4). We are told to be likeminded (Phil 2:2) and to work hard to build and maintain unity: "Make every effort to keep the unity of the Spirit through the bond of peace. There is one body and one Spirit— just as you were called to one hope when you were called— one Lord, one faith, one baptism; one God and Father of all, who is over all and through all and in all" (Eph 4:3-6). This relational unity is based on the foundation of unity in our common faith in Christ.

So if the circle is those who will be in glory with us, worshipping the crucified and risen Jesus for all eternity, and that includes all those in churches all around us—even though they have a different name on the building and sing from a different hymnbook—what might it look like to the watching world if we found ways to reflect that organic unity in a visible way?

Wouldn't it be great if we are known for our love for each other instead of our divisions? Wouldn't it be great if we were known for authentically loving each other despite our differences, known for working together to love and serve our neighbors with outrageous,

---

[43] *ibid*, 267.

gracious, liberal generosity? Francis Chan writes "We need to stop giving people excuses not to believe in God. You've probably heard the expression, 'I believe in God, just not organized religion.' I don't think people would say that if the church truly lived like we are called to live. The expression would change to 'I can't deny what the church does, but I don't believe in their God.' At least then they'd address their rejection of God rather than use the church as a scapegoat."[44]

So what could that look like? In Rhode Island, dozens of churches have crossed over denominational lines and banded together around the state in the "Love RI" effort to bring Jesus to their neighbors. Using the "Prayer-Care-Share" model, these churches meet together multiple times each year to pray for their neighbors, then mount community-wide projects to serve their neighbors, and finally to transition to sharing the reason for their love and care, the love and care of Jesus. This multi-church, cross-denominational effort came directly from relationships first forged in the Greater RI Area Pastors' Prayer Summit. This annual three-day prayer retreat began in 2006 and is open to all pastors in the greater RI area. Each spring dozens of these pastors from evangelical and pentecostal, conservative and charismatic, liturgical and informal/contemporary churches meet with no other agenda than prayer and worship. And out of those times of prayer have come lowered suspicions and healed relationships, new understandings and tight friendships.

And what is happening in Rhode Island is just one chapter of a larger story of what God is doing in 21 cities around the country like Branson, Missouri and Cedar Rapids, Iowa; small cities like Newton, Kansas and large cities like Phoenix, Arizona; in Fresno, California on the west coast, El Paso, Texas in the south, up north in Fox Valley, Illinois and of course, RI on the Atlantic coast in the Northeast. Under the umbrella of *LC2C* (Loving our Communities to Christ),[45] this effort celebrates the love and unity of followers of Jesus from many different

---

[44] Francis Chan, *Crazy Love: Overwhelmed by a relentless God* (Colorado Springs: David C. Cook, 2008), p. 5.

[45] Check out the story and work of the *Mission America Coalition*, the parent organization behind *LC2C*, at www.missionamerica.org.

denominations and traditions in one city and capitalizes on their combined strength and resources to impact whole communities with the gospel.

Locally, *Good News Bible Chapel* (with our Plymouth Brethren heritage) has teamed up with *Faith Alliance Church* (Christian Missionary Alliance), *South Attleboro Assembly of God* (AoG), and *Iglesia Vida Nueva de Attleboro* (Independent) in the *Saltshaker*[46] project to display the unity and love of followers of Jesus in "The Church of Attleboro" while loving and serving our neighbors. And this effort came directly from the relationships built in the weekly prayer breakfast for Attleboro area pastors who recognize themselves as "the elders of the church of Attleboro."

This story of choosing to value love and unity for the sake of the gospel over denominational/movement distinctives and historic traditions is repeated in many cities and towns, not just across America but around the world, as followers of Christ begin to love each other and boldly display that love and unity in the face of a fractured and broken culture.

> *Dear friends, let us love one another, for love comes from God.*
> *Everyone who loves has been born of God and knows God.*
> *Whoever does not love does not know God, because God is love.*
> *This is how God showed his love among us: He sent his one and only Son*
> *into the world that we might live through him.*
> *This is love: not that we loved God, but that he loved us and sent*
> *his Son as an atoning sacrifice for our sins.*
> *Dear friends, since God so loved us, we also ought to love one another.*
> *No one has ever seen God; but if we love one another,*
> *God lives in us and his love is made complete in us.*
> *– 1 John 4:7-12*

---

[46] See Chapter 10 for more details on this multi-church, cross-denominational *Saltshaker* ministry — "Unifying the church of Attleboro to love the city of Attleboro" — of prayer, practical and generous love and compassion and gospel proclamation.

Digging deeper...

- Assignment: Read John 13:34, 35 and John 17:20, 21 out loud each day for one week. Use those words to turn those verses into your personal prayer to God each day.

- What do you think the *value* is for all of us in the very different traditions and distinctives of different denominations and movements?

- How can you love and work with Christians who will be in heaven with you — but who you disagree with on one topic or doctrine or another?

- What would it look like in your city/town/village if the Christians of different churches worked together to love and serve their neighbors? What has to change in your situation to make that happen? What can you do to help initiate that change?

CHAPTER 10

...and love your neighbor

"Which of these three do you think was a neighbor to the man who fell into the hands of robbers?" The expert in the law replied, "The one who had mercy on him." Jesus told him, "Go and do likewise."
- Luke 10:36, 37

"Love the Lord your God with all your heart and with all your soul and with all your mind and with all your strength. The second is this: love your neighbor as yourself."
- Mark 12:30

When a rich young man approached Jesus and asked how he could be assured of heaven when he died (Luke 10:25-37), Jesus responded, as he frequently did, with a question: "What is written in the Law?" he replied, "How do you read it?" (Jesus was talking there of the entire 613 Mitzvah of the Jewish Old Testament Law outlined by Moses.) At this question the young man answered by quoting the essence of the Law of Moses from Deuteronomy 6:5 and Leviticus 19:18: "'Love the Lord your God with all your heart and with all your soul and with all your strength and with all your mind'; and, 'Love your neighbor as yourself.'" So Jesus challenged him with the statement "You have answered correctly. Do this and you will live." To this the rich man responded "And who is my neighbor?" because, the text reveals, he wanted to justify himself, apparently prove that he was good enough before God to "inherit eternal life."

Jesus responded with the story that we know as "The Good Samaritan," describing a man who fell into a trap laid by thieves as he travelled down the hillside from Jerusalem to the nearby city of Jericho. Robbed, beaten and left for dead at the roadside, the man was seen by a few who passed by. First, a priest saw him, and then crossed to the other side of the road (maybe so that he was not made "unclean" and unable to serve in the temple by touching what he possibly feared might be a dead body). Next a Levite saw the victim, but he also made a wide path around him, maybe to also avoid ceremonial uncleanness. Finally, a man from Samaria saw the victim, stopped to help him and even brought him to an inn where he could be cared for until he recovered, even paying for all the expenses.

At which point Jesus asked the rich young man, "Which of these three do you think was a neighbor to the man who fell into the hands of robbers?" The expert in the law replied, "The one who had mercy on him." Jesus told him, "Go and do likewise."

The point of this poignant story, you remember, was about obeying the two greatest commands: "Love God and love your neighbor." The two commands are inseparable. Maybe that is because our neighbors are made in the very image of God (Genesis 1:27) and as such they have intrinsic worth and loving them is in some way intricately tied to loving God. Or, to put it in the negative: ignoring, despising, rejecting our neighbors, is in some way incompatible with saying that we love God.

The fact that the hero of this carefully crafted story that Jesus told was from the region of Samaria is central to the point. The Jews of Jesus' day despised the Samaritans for two reasons. They considered people from Samaria to be racial half-breeds because their ancestors were left behind as too poor to bother with when the Jewish aristocracy was carried away into the captivity in Babylon starting in 586BC and subsequently they had intermarried with other transplanted foreigners. Second, they were loathed as religious compromisers who followed only the Torah, the first five books of the Hebrew Bible, and worshipped, not in the Temple in Jerusalem with other Jews, but on a hilltop at Gerizim in Samaria. So the fact that this rejected outcast was the rescuer who cared for the wounded sufferer when his "religious" road-mates did not is important to notice. It must have irked the listening Pharisees that in Jesus' story, it was this social outcast who demonstrated obedience to the Mitzvah to "love your neighbor," not the two Law-obsessed religious leaders.

If we are to obey the command of Jesus to love our neighbors, it is important that we force ourselves to reflect on, just as this rich young man was compelled to consider, who our neighbor really is. It is easy to love people like us. It is considerably more difficult to deliberately choose to love those who are different from us, maybe by their language or skin color, by their social class or economic status, maybe different from us by their culture or their education. Actually, to be honest, many of those in need are not very lovable. Some are downright scary.

Jesus has set a powerful example for us, in a very dramatic way, in loving our neighbors who are difficult to love. Look at the gospel[47] by Mark chapter 5, beginning at verse 2: "When Jesus got out of the boat, a man with an evil spirit came from the tombs to meet him. This man lived in the tombs, and no one could bind him any more, not even with a chain. For he had often been chained hand and foot, but he tore the chains apart and broke the irons on his feet. No one was strong enough to subdue him. Night and day among the tombs and in the hills he would cry out and cut himself with stones." This guy's life was horrible! He was the poster child for misery! A homeless outcast from his community, he was living alone in a graveyard. I suspect no one cared for him, no one visited him; even his own family disowned him. Hurt and wounded by those in authority, he hurt and wounded himself even more. Verse 6: "When he saw Jesus from a distance, he ran and fell on his knees in front of him. He shouted at the top of his voice, "What do you want with me, Jesus, Son of the Most High God? Swear to God that you won't torture me!" What does that mean, "Swear to God that you won't torture me!"? I think it means "Don't hurt me, Jesus. I'm already broken and hurting

---

[47] "Gospel" simply means "good news, from the Greek, *evangelion*. The four "Gospels" are four accounts of the life and ministry of Jesus, i.e., the good news about Jesus.

enough. I'm already wrecked by violence and anger and sin; I don't need more anger, Jesus; everybody already hates me for who I am and what I've done, Jesus, I even hate myself; I don't need more hate; I'm already despised, rejected, abused, Jesus. If you're not going to help me, then at least please don't hurt me more! Jesus, I'm lonely and afraid and broken—please don't give me what I deserve; show me mercy, Jesus!" And the text tells us that Jesus cast out the evil spirits and healed the man. Talk about loving the unlovable!

This story makes me think of the times I avoid the drunken bum lying on the street, walk around the smelly beggar asking for change—avoid the misfits of our community—all because they make me feel uncomfortable. It makes me think of those I know are deep in sin, some by choice; all by habit. I see many people all around us who have been badly hurt by the ones that they trusted, the ones who were supposed to love them and care for them and protect them—maybe their family, and in some cases, maybe the church. Others have chosen a path of deliberate disobedience and open rebellion, thinking that their independence from God would bring pleasure and joy. But usually it just brings misery and pain: "The pleasures of sin last for a season..." (Hebrews 11:25).

And too often my response to seeing them is a callous, "They deserve what they are getting." Too often I am waiting for them to clean up their act and begin to demonstrate righteousness. Too often I look down at them in judgment, even if I know better than to say anything judgmental out loud. I confess that I feel inwardly superior in my righteous indignation at their sin.

The demon possessed man feared, surely from his experience with religious people, receiving any more anger and hatred. But instead, Jesus set him free. Physically, mentally, and spiritually.

"Oh Father, forgive me for condemning to the loneliness of rejection those who need your mercy and grace. Oh that I would have the tender and compassionate heart of Jesus and the eyes of Jesus for the poor and broken of our city, the wounded and

despised all around us, and offer them healing and forgiveness in Jesus' name."

But be sure that you do not miss a secondary point of the Good Samaritan story. The account focused on the very real physical needs of the bruised victim. The "spiritual" ones, the priest and the Levite, just passed by him, avoiding any contact. The one who showed the love of God to the victim actually took time to clean and bandage his wounds, interrupted his own trip to bring the wounded traveler to an inn and get him settled. This example points us all to the intentional investment of our time and resources to love our neighbor in practical, life-saving, life-changing ways. Not all of us will have the opportunity to serve the victim of a robbery. Not all of us will be in the right place at the right time to be a hero. But each of us needs to live life loosely, loose enough so that we can interrupt what we are doing and take the time to help the neighbor in need, to clean out and bind up physical and emotional and spiritual wounds.

In our culture of fast moving schedules run by our Blackberry™ calendars and the imperatives of family and work and sports and church and it takes a deliberate choice to be obedient to the command of Jesus to "love your neighbor." What might that look like? In 1984 a group of Christians, obedient Jesus followers, in the city of Portland, Maine (Greater Portland's population is around 640,000) noticed that the teens of their neighborhood were getting into trouble after school with gangs and drugs, and certainly not getting any schoolwork done. They decided to serve the students through an after-school drop-in center. The initial facility wasn't very fancy or cool. Actually, it was a fixed-up, dirt-floor basement in a Mennonite church. Nothing special. Just genuine Christ-love for neighbors. Today, *The Root Cellar* ministry is a multi-church effort in Portland and nearby Lewiston, Maine, providing a long list of free services to their neighbors in the name of Jesus. The hundreds of volunteers involved must give clear testimony to a saving relationship with Jesus Christ. And the gospel is central to the conversations and relationships that are at the core of *The Root Cellar's* work. And about a thousand miles west, a few disciples of Jesus in the town of Bradford, Ontario (pop. 24,000) saw unmet needs in their community in 2001 and brought together what is now seven churches in a cross-denominational, community-service effort called *Cross Trainers Ministries*. Through *CrossTrainers*, local Christ-followers provide an after-school drop-in center, a transitional home for women and children at risk, free clothing and food, all in the name of Jesus.

Ironically—actually, it is so obviously a "God-thing" that it still stuns me today—a short-term missions team from *Faith Alliance Church* in my small city of Attleboro (population: 42,000) served for a week in the summer of 2010 in Portland, with *The Root Cellar* team. And at the same time, a short-term missions team from Good News served with *CrossTrainiers* in Bradford. When pastor Don Wigand of *Faith Alliance* and I compared stories over breakfast a few days after the teams returned, we were both struck at how God had dramatically worked in those projects and how both of us were prompted by the Spirit to ask *"Why can't we serve our neighbors in Attleboro in the name of Jesus the same way?"* Out of that breakfast conversation and much prayer has come a multi-church, cross-denominational compassion ministry called *The Saltshaker*, demonstrating the unity of the Bride of Christ and showing the love of God in practical ways to our neighbors in need in Attleboro.

While loving our neighbors with the life-saving gospel of Jesus is central to the mission and work of the scores of obedient Christ-followers at *The Root Cellar, CrossTrainers Ministries*, and *The Saltshaker*, there is a clear, simple Biblical mandate for loving our neighbors based on the heart of God. Look at Isaiah 58:3. The first five verses of the chapter open with the children of Israel asking why their fasting and their religious rituals are not acceptable to God:

> Why have we fasted, and you see it not? Why have we humbled ourselves, and you take no knowledge of it? (And then God explained to his chosen people once again what his heart is all about and what kind of "religion" he really desires.

In a powerful, powerful declaration God outlined what it means to love our neighbors...) Is not this the fast that I choose: to loose the bonds of wickedness, to undo the straps of the yoke, to let the oppressed go free, and to break every yoke? Is it not to share your bread with the hungry and bring the homeless poor into your house; when you see the naked, to cover him, and not to hide yourself from your own flesh? Then shall your light break forth like the dawn, and your healing shall spring up speedily; your righteousness shall go before you; the glory of the LORD shall be your rear guard. Then you shall call, and the LORD will answer; you shall cry, and he will say, 'Here I am.' If you take away the yoke from your midst, the pointing of the finger, and speaking wickedness, if you pour yourself out for the hungry and satisfy the desire of the afflicted, then shall your light rise in the darkness and your gloom be as the noonday. And the LORD will guide you continually and satisfy your desire in scorched places and make your bones strong; and you shall be like a watered garden, like a spring of water, whose waters do not fail. And your ancient ruins shall be rebuilt you shall raise up the foundations of many generations; you shall be called the repairer of the breach, the restorer of streets to dwell in.

You and I, as obedient disciples of Jesus, are called to love our neighbors, and not just the lovable, friendly ones like us who look good and smell good and do good. Pray that God will open your eyes to the needs of your neighbors and that you will obey his command: "Love the Lord your God with all your heart, with all your soul, and with all your mind; and love your neighbor as yourself."

Digging deeper...

● Read again the passage from Isaiah chapter 58 that is quoted above. Read also Isaiah 1:11-17. Which do you think God values more, worship or justice? Why?

● Read Proverbs 21:3 1, James 1:27 and 1 Peter 2:12. How are loving your neighbor and doing acts of justice both acts of worship that are pleasing and acceptable to God?

● Life is busy. I get it. So how can you structure your hectic life so that there is time to show your neighbors that you love them by serving them in generous and practical ways? Write down a couple of ideas of what that might look like, then pray for God to show you what he is already doing that you can be part of...

CHAPTER 11

Command #6:

Give

"Do not store up for yourselves treasures on earth, where moth and rust destroy, and where thieves break in and steal. But store up for yourselves treasures in heaven, where moth and rust do not destroy, and where thieves do not break in and steal. For where your treasure is, there your heart will be also."

- Matthew 6:19-21

In the summer of 2010 Warren Buffet and Bill Gates, the two richest billionaires in America, got a copy of the *Forbes 400*, the Forbes magazine list of the 400 richest people in America. Then they divided up the list, got on the phone and started to call each one of them—who wouldn't take a call from Bill Gates or Warren Buffet? I'm not really sure what the calls went like. I'm guessing something like, "Hi Jim (talking to Jim Walton, co-heir of the Walmart fortune), Hey Jim, this is Warren. How's it going? Bought any small countries lately?" No, actually, it was reported that Bill and Warren started to call the Top 400 richest people in America and challenged them to each give away half of their fortune before they died. And after only 80 phone calls, 38 of the richest men and women in America agreed to give away 50% or more of their fortune to charity before they died. NYC Mayor and media tycoon Michael Bloomberg, entertainment titan Barry Diller, Oracle co-founder Larry Ellison, energy tycoon T. Boone Pickens, media mogul Ted Turner, rich guy David Rockefeller, film director George Lucas, the list goes on.

The 38 names that pledged initially had a combined net worth surpassing $230 billion. And they agreed to give half of it away before they die. Gates and Buffet practice what they preach: Warren already has pledged to give away 99% of his multi-billion dollar fortune before he died, most of it to *The Bill and Melinda Gates Charitable Foundation*! Michael Bloomberg said "You don't want to leave so much money (to your kids) that it ruins their lives." The point is, they see money not as a thing to collect and hoard but as a tool to be put to work; a tool to accomplish something of bigger value, more lasting value than the tool itself.

So far we've looked at five of the basic commands of Jesus that every disciple, every Christ-follower should know, and more importantly—if we want to be actually considered an authentic disciple of Jesus—five basic commands of Jesus that every disciple should obey. Just before he returned to heaven, Jesus told the eleven disciples to "Go and make disciples of all nations, baptizing them in the name of the Father and of the Son and of the Holy Spirit, and teaching them to obey everything I have commanded you."

The first command we looked at was the command to Repent and Believe. The second was Be Baptized. The third was Remember Me. The fourth was Pray. The fifth was Love God, Each Other, and Neighbor. The sixth foundational command for all disciples of Jesus is found in the gospel by Matthew 6—the first book of the New Testament—Matthew, chapter 6, verse 19: "Do not store up for yourselves treasures on earth, where moth and rust destroy, and where thieves break in and steal. But store up for yourselves treasures in heaven, where moth and rust do not destroy, and where thieves do not break in and steal. For where your treasure is, there your heart will be also." The command here is the command by Jesus to give.

In his small but excellent book *The Treasure Principle*, Randy Alcorn breaks these verses down into simple concepts regarding money.[48] First

---

[48] Randy Alcorn *The Treasure Principle: Unlocking the secret of joyful giving.* (Colorado Springs: WaterBrook/Multnomah, 2005).

he says, this text tells us "Don't renounce treasure; relocate it!" Notice in verse 19 that Jesus said "Do not store up for yourselves treasures on earth, where moth and rust destroy, and where thieves break in and steal. But store up for yourselves treasures in heaven..." Work for something that will really last, something that is bigger than you, something that really matters. In their own way, Bill Gates, Warren Buffet and the other 38 billionaires are trying to do that. But Jesus said that there are some things that transcend this life. They last for eternity. Some things impact eternal destinies; some things that change everything forever! And Jesus says that's where you should be putting your treasure!

Second, notice in verse 21 that Jesus said "For where your treasure is, there your heart will be also." Alcorn restates it this way: "My heart always goes where I put God's money."

Do you want to know where your heart *really* is? Just look where you spend your money. Your credit card statement tells all. Your checkbook statement reveals everything. Alcorn points out that the good news of this principle is very simple and very powerful. *Your heart will naturally go wherever you put your treasure!* If your heart is not in a good place now—if you reflect and discover that you are selfish, materialistic, too obsessed with the newest, biggest, fastest, coolest, too focused on collecting and keeping score of your toys—you can change all that by putting your money where your heart should be. Agree to regularly support a missionary. Support a child monthly through *World Vision* or *Compassion International.* Help a third-world family become self-sufficient through micro-lending (check out www.microseeds.org). Donate to a soup kitchen or women's shelter. Offer a scholarship to a Christian summer camp for a kid who couldn't go otherwise. Buy a box of paperback bibles for the Rescue Mission. Start putting your money in the right places and—surprise, surprise—your heart will follow!

Let's spend a few minutes unpacking the *Why*. Why give? What's the reason; what's the motivation to give? Well, obviously in this book, the first reason that you and I, as obedient followers of Jesus, should faithfully and sacrificially give is because Jesus told us to, right here in

Matthew 6:19-21! To give is to obey Jesus! And that's what Jesus-loving, Christ-followers do! We obey his commands!

But I suspect that the second answer to that "Why give" question is not what you think. I'm not going to talk about all the good that can be done with "The 3-Ts," your time, your treasure and your talents. I want you to step back and see the real reason why we should give. And it is because *our God is a giver!* Think for a moment about John 3:16, that "gospel in a nutshell" verse that you should know by memory: "For God so loved the world that he gave his one and only Son..." Then there's 1 John 5:11: "God has given us eternal life, and this life is in his Son." God has given "...to all who received him, to those who believed in his name... the right to become children of God" (John 1:12). God "has given us new birth into a living hope through the resurrection of Jesus Christ from the dead" (1 Peter 1:3). John 3:34 tells us that God the Father gives the Holy Spirit to us without limit (2 Corinthians 5:5). God gives us the gift of faith (Romans 12:3). God gives us his grace (1 Corinthians 1:4; 2 Corinthians 8:9). God gives you "...the Spirit of wisdom and revelation, so that you may know him better" (Ephesians 1:17; James 1:5). God "by his grace gave us eternal encouragement and good hope" (2 Thessalonians 2:16). God gives us "a spirit of power, of love and of self-discipline" (2 Timothy 1:7). In fact, "his divine power has given us *everything we need for life and godliness* through our knowledge of him who called us by his own glory and goodness" (2 Peter 1:3). God the Father is a giver! His children should reflect their Father. God is a giver; you should be a giver, too.

God the Father is a giver and Jesus the Son is a giver. The apostle Paul writes in Galatians 2:20 "I have been crucified with Christ and I no longer live, but Christ lives in me. The life I live in the body, I live by faith in the Son of God, who loved me and gave Himself for me." "Christ loved us and gave Himself up for us as a fragrant offering and sacrifice to God" (Ephesians 5:2). "Christ loved the church and gave Himself up for her to make her holy, cleansing her by the washing with water through the word, and to present her to Himself as a radiant church, without stain or wrinkle or any other blemish, but holy and blameless" (Ephesians 5:25ff).

God the Father is a giver. Jesus the Son is a giver. And, the Holy Spirit is a giver. 1 Corinthians chapter 12 tells us that the Holy Spirit is the giver of *charisma*, spiritual gifts that equip believers to serve each other in the family of God. Second Corinthians chapter 3, verse 6: it is the Spirit who gives us new life. 1 Thessalonians 1:6: it is the Holy Spirit that gives us joy.

Why should we give? First, because Jesus commanded us to give. Second, because, God the Father is as giver. Jesus the Son is a giver. The Holy Spirit is a giver. So you see the picture? The whole Trinity is engaged in giving. Giving generously. Giving graciously. Giving without expecting anything in return. Giving first: before we even repent, before we even believe, God is initiating the giving. When you give, you are reflecting the heart of the Father, the heart of Jesus, the gifts of the Spirit.

You are called to be a giver, not a taker. Now I know that some are in a different financial position, in a different life circumstance than others. There is no shame in receiving gifts when you are in genuine need. That's what the early church did (see Acts 4:32). That's one way that we can demonstrate love for God and neighbor, by giving to meet the needs of others, particularly those of the household of faith. "As we have therefore opportunity, let us do good unto all men, especially unto them who are of the household of faith." (Galatians 6:10). So clearly there is no shame in receiving gifts when you are in genuine need.

But let me say that if you are not in a position to give now, then your job is to work hard to get to a place where you *can* give instead of taking. If you are just starting out on your career after school, then your goal in life should be working to become a giver. *That* will be success. If you are just starting out after a major life-change, recovering from a divorce, just getting out of prison or rehab, maybe for you it's just beginning retirement—whatever your life-change circumstances—your goal should be to become a giver. If you are up to your neck in debt, your goal should be getting out of debt as soon as possible so that you can become a giver. (Not so that you can get a bigger TV or qualify for another credit card.) If you are already making some good money and wondering what your next purchase or investment should be, then you need to become a giver. If your lifestyle is eating up all that you earn, and maybe a little more, then your goal is to simplify and downsize so that you can become a giver.

Why? Because God, your Father in heaven, is a giver. Jesus, the Savior of your soul, is a giver. The Holy Spirit, that great Comforter, is a giver. You should reflect the character of the Father, the Son and the Spirit and be a giver.

Digging deeper...

- Since "Your heart follows your treasure," where is your heart right now? Where would you like it to be? Take some time now to pray about that. Write down any thoughts that the Holy Spirit brings to mind as you pray.

- God is a giver. Jesus is a giver. The Holy Spirit is a giver. How can you be a generous giver like God? Write down the ways you can become a giver of your Time, your Talent and your Treasure.

- My Time

- My Talent

- My Treasure

- Assignment: Write out Matthew 6:19-21 on a card and memorize these verses, with their text "address."

CHAPTER 12

Command #7:
Make Disciples

"Therefore go and make disciples of all nations."
- Matthew 28:19

"And the things you have heard me say in the presence of many witnesses entrust to reliable men who will also be qualified to teach others."
- 2 Timothy 2:2

In the opening lines of his missions classic *Let The Nations Be Glad!*, John Piper wrote "Missions exist because worship doesn't."[49] Our God is a missionary God. He wants women and men and students and children everywhere—of every language, of every race, of every cultural group—to worship him. And the Bible tells us that ultimately people of every language and tribe and nation will fall down and worship him (Philippians 2:9-11).

Command number 6 is right in the middle of our "Obeying Jesus" text, Matthew 28:19: "Therefore go and make disciples of all nations…" It couldn't be plainer. The final command of Jesus to the 11 disciples was to "Go and … make disciples." Grow. Multiply. Proliferate. Reproduce yourself. You and I sit here today because they were obedient to that

---

[49] Piper, John. *Let The Nations Be Glad: The supremacy of God in missions* (Ada, Michigan: Baker Academic, 2nd edition, 2003), 17.

command. They made disciples, baptizing them in the name of the Father, the Son and the Holy Spirit and teaching them to obey everything that Jesus commanded. When you read the book of Acts, you find that they did it pretty quickly, under pressure of persecution. The honeymoon period in Jerusalem following Jesus' ascension lasted a few months at best before the persecution began and they were scattered in Judea, Samaria and ultimately all the ends of the earth (See Acts 8:1ff). Phillip reached out the eunuch from Ethiopia. John-Mark went deep into Egypt. Church history tells us that Thomas, the one we call Doubting Thomas, went all the way through Syria and the Persian Empire to what was then the Indo-Parthian Empire, known today as India and Pakistan, with the gospel of Jesus Christ, making disciples all along the way.

Others spread out throughout the Roman Empire. The apostle Paul brought the gospel to Turkey, Greece and Italy. And as they were going, they made disciples. Jesus said that making disciples would include two basic tasks: baptizing the disciples in the name of the Father, the Son and the Holy Spirit; and second, teaching them to obey everything that he had commanded. Telling someone about Jesus is only the first half of the job. That's like teaching your kid how to ride a bike without teaching them how to use the brakes. That's like learning to kick a soccer ball but never learning the rules of the game. That's like making a grilled cheese sandwich, carefully preparing and grilling the bread, without adding the cheese. That's a job half-done.

8 lessons in making disciples from the life of Jesus...

The complete assignment is telling them about Jesus *and* discipling that new believer. How do you do that? How do you make a disciple? We can learn from the best-practices example of the master disciple-maker, Jesus. Let me use the word "Disciple" to show you 8 lessons in discipling from the life of Jesus.

The first lesson we can learn about making disciples from the life of Jesus is the letter "D" for *Do Life Together*. Look at John 2:1, 2: "On the third day a wedding took place at Cana in Galilee. Jesus' mother was there, and Jesus and his disciples had also been invited to the wedding."

John tells us here that just three days into his public ministry, Jesus was hanging out with his disciples at a wedding. That's where they observed him doing his first miracle. Look at Luke, chapter 8, verse 1: "After this, Jesus traveled about from one town and village to another, proclaiming the good news of the kingdom of God. The Twelve were with him..." As Jesus went around the towns and villages, teaching, healing the sick and feeding the hungry, proclaiming the good news of the Kingdom of God, the core twelve traveled with him. Verse two in chapter 8 tells us that a number of women were travelling with them as well. Doing life together. Look at Matthew 26, verse 36: "Then Jesus went with his disciples to a place called Gethsemane, and he said to them, "Sit here while I go over there and pray." At the very beginning of his ministry, during the travels all over Israel when he was busy and popular, and even in the difficult final days leading up to his arrest, trial and crucifixion, Jesus took them with him; they did life together.

The first way that you can make disciples is by letting those that you have a discipling relationship with see you doing life; the good times, the difficult times—experiencing life together. When you go to visit someone in the hospital, take your disciple with you. When you go to your midweek small group, take your disciple with you. When you go serve at the soup kitchen or at the local nursing home, take your disciple with you. When you work on reroofing the shed or sewing new curtains, take your disciple along for the experience. Do life together. That's what Jesus did.

And what are you doing while you're doing life together? That's the letter "I," use the opportunity to *Instruct in Truth & Scripture*. That's what Jesus did. Look at Mark chapter 4. Mark 4, start at verse 33: "With many similar parables Jesus spoke the word to them, as much as they could understand. He did not say anything to them without using a parable. But when he was alone with his own disciples, he explained everything." They did more than talk about the news and weather or how the fishing was at Galilee. Jesus used stories from life and then applied spiritual principles to them—we call them parables. "They were on their way up to Jerusalem, with Jesus leading the way, and the disciples were astonished, while those who followed were afraid. Again he took the Twelve aside and told them what was going to happen to him" (Mark 10:32). I like the word "again" there; "*Again* he took the Twelve aside and told them what was going to happen to him." Constant teaching—instructing in truth and scripture.

Let me raise a caution here about teaching and instructing. Many are afraid of the whole idea of making a disciple: "I don't know enough theology! I don't have Bible verses memorized! I don't know the answers to the tough questions about Bible doctrine!" Others, usually those who are teachers by gifting, those who best understand things that are systematic and structured, immediately think of discipleship in terms of downloading data; the more *information* the new disciple gets, the better! But making a disciple of Jesus is not about teaching theology or doctrine or history or quoting Bible memory verses. Making disciples is about "teaching them to obey all that I have commanded." Knowledge-based discipleship (theology, history, doctrine, Bible memory) produces Christ-followers with head-knowledge that all too often never connects to the heart, the emotions, the attitudes or the behaviors. But obedience-based discipleship teaches disciples to obey Jesus first,[50] and then let the knowledge of theology and doctrine and Bible memory come along and fill in the gaps.

That brings us to our third lesson in discipling from the life of Jesus: "S" for *Seize the Teachable Moment.* Seize the teachable moment. Look over at Luke chapter 24; look down starting at verse 25, the story of Jesus after his resurrection on the road to the village of Emmaus:

> He said to them, "How foolish you are, and how slow of heart to believe all that the prophets have spoken! Did not the Christ have to suffer these things and then enter his glory?" And beginning with Moses and all the Prophets, he explained to them what was said in all the Scriptures concerning Himself.

---

[50] It is profitable to read the brief article on "Obedience Based Discipleship" by David Watson, a seasoned church planter and trainer of church planters found at http://www.davidwatson.org/ 2007/08/20/obedience-based-discipleship

As they approached the village to which they were going, Jesus acted as if he were going farther. But they urged him strongly, "Stay with us, for it is nearly evening; the day is almost over." So he went in to stay with them. When he was at the table with them, he took bread, gave thanks, broke it and began to give it to them. Then their eyes were opened and they recognized him, and he disappeared from their sight. They asked each other, "Were not our hearts burning within us while he talked with us on the road and opened the Scriptures to us?"

Jesus took advantage of the situation; he used the circumstances and seized the opportunity to teach. I know that I'm usually too absorbed in the moment, too focused on myself, to notice that _this_ is the chance, _this_ is the moment to use the situation as a teaching opportunity. Particularly when things aren't going according to my plan, I miss the opportunity to apply a spiritual lesson. Jesus didn't.

Look at Mark 9:33-35, Mark, chapter 9, look at verse 33: "They came to Capernaum. When he was in the house, he asked them, 'What were you arguing about on the road?' But they kept quiet because on the way they had argued about who was the greatest. Sitting down, Jesus called the Twelve and said, 'If anyone wants to be first, he must be the very last, and the servant of all.'" He deliberately, consciously used their argument as a teaching opportunity. He seized the teachable moment.

That leads us to the next lesson, "C" for _Correct Without Delay_. Jesus would not let untruth go unchallenged or bad attitudes go unchecked. "But when Jesus turned and looked at his disciples, he rebuked Peter, 'Get behind me, Satan!' he said. 'You do not have in mind the things of God, but the things of men'" (Mark 8:33). Jesus wouldn't let something that was wrong just pass without comment, just to keep the peace. He wouldn't ignore mistakes, even when it meant a public rebuke. Because Peter had spoken publically, Jesus rebuked him publically. He didn't take Peter aside privately to straighten him out because that would have left everyone else with just the wrong impression and no correction.

I remember Bill Hybels telling about a particular meeting that they had at Willow Creek Community Church where a woman got up and spoke out pretty sharply, pretty abusively. Bill stopped her—in front of everyone—and asked her to restate what she was saying in a more gracious and loving way. He didn't let it pass. Her public behavior was corrected gently but publically so all could learn the lesson, so no one would leave thinking that kind of participation was acceptable. Jesus consistently set the example for us to follow: "People were bringing little children to Jesus to have him touch them, but the disciples rebuked them. When Jesus saw this, he was indignant. He said to them, "Let the little children come to me, and do not hinder them, for the kingdom of God belongs to such as these" (Mark 10:13-16). Jesus would not let untruth go uncorrected. He wouldn't ignore it and hope they learned later. Even his dearest friends would be gently rebuked when necessary. "'Martha, Martha,' the Lord answered, 'you are worried and upset about many things, but only one thing is needed. Mary has chosen what is better, and it will not be taken away from her'" (Luke 10:41). Jesus publically challenged Martha, but he called her by name and did it affectionately, warmly, so that she could never doubt that he cared deeply for her. And he corrected without delay.

The next lesson from the best practice of discipling by Jesus is the letter "I" for *Involve Others*. Jesus was always including others, rarely dealing with just one disciple at a time.

> As Jesus was walking beside the Sea of Galilee, he saw two brothers, Simon called Peter and his brother Andrew. They were casting a net into the lake, for they were fishermen. "Come, follow me," Jesus said, "and I will make you fishers of men." At once they left their nets and followed him. Going on from there, he saw two other brothers, James son of Zebedee and his brother John. They were in a boat with their father Zebedee, preparing their nets. Jesus called them, and immediately they left the boat and their father and followed him. (Matthew 4:18-22)

If you are going to invest your time and effort in discipling someone, take a few others along on the journey and multiply the results of your effort. That's what Jesus did. "After this the Lord appointed seventy-two others and sent them two by two ahead of him to every town and place where he was about to go" (Luke 10:1). If you are spending a lot of time with just a few, it's easy for them to get to think that somehow they're special. The best way to level that natural feeling is to occasionally involve others in one of your experiences. It humbles your disciples. It blesses the ones you're engaging and it exposes them to your discipling efforts. That's what Jesus did; Involve Others.

The next lesson is critical. The letter P stands for *Pray*. First, we saw earlier that Jesus prayed before he invited his disciples to join him. "One of those days Jesus went out to a mountainside to pray, and spent the night praying to God. When morning came, he called his disciples to him and chose twelve of them, whom he also designated apostles" (Luke 6:12). Jesus didn't wait for them to choose him; he chose them. And he prayed for them even before he chose them. You should too. Near the end of his ministry, we find Jesus with the disciples on the night that he was betrayed. Simon Peter had just boasted that *he* would never deny that he knew Jesus. Jesus replied: "Simon, Simon, Satan has asked to sift you as wheat. But I have prayed for you, Simon, that your faith may not fail. And when you have turned back, strengthen your brothers" (Luke 22:31-33). So second, Jesus prayed that the faith of his disciples would never fail. You can pray that prayer for your disciples. And later in the Garden, Jesus prayed for his disciples—and for us!

> I pray for them. I am not praying for the world, but for those you have given me, for they are yours. All I have is yours, and all you have is mine. And glory has come to me through them. I will remain in the world no longer, but they are still in the world, and I am coming to you. Holy Father, protect them by the power of your name—the name you gave me—so that they may be one as we are one. While I was with them, I protected them and kept them safe by that name you gave me.

None has been lost except the one doomed to destruction so that Scripture would be fulfilled. I am coming to you now, but I say these things while I am still in the world, so that they may have the full measure of my joy within them. I have given them your word and the world has hated them, for they are not of the world any more than I am of the world. My prayer is not that you take them out of the world but that you protect them from the evil one (John 17: 20-26).

Third, did you just notice in that prayer that Jesus prayed for their protection. You can pray for your disciples' protection from temptation, from the lure of worldliness, from the attacks of the evil one. From the beginning to the end—from your choosing disciples, your investment in them, and even at the conclusion of your time together—all of it should be soaked in prayer. That's what Jesus did.

Two more lessons. First, the letter "L" stands for *Lead by Example*. Look back at Luke, Luke chapter 11, verse 1: "One day Jesus was praying in a certain place. When he finished, one of his disciples said to him, "Lord, teach us to pray, just as John taught his disciples." His example, praying where they could watch him and hear him, praying in front of them, stimulated their desire to learn and grow in their own prayer life. You can expose your disciple to the disciplines of prayer and Bible study, worship and serving, by doing it in front of them, letting them observe him in action. In the report of Jesus and the woman at the well in John 4:27ff, we have the classic example of leading by example. "Just then his disciples returned and were surprised to find him talking with a woman. But no one asked, 'What do you want?' or 'Why are you talking with her?'" The disciples, like most Jewish men of their time and culture, would not have anything to do with a person from Samaria, considered religious infidels and cultural half-breeds. And they wouldn't have anything to do with a woman in public, particularly a woman of such low reputation as this one. And they find Jesus not only having a conversation with her, but a conversation about delicate personal matters and deep spiritual issues. He didn't have to give them a theoretical lecture in reaching out to the marginalized and despised of society. He didn't have to teach them about leaving your comfort zone to ignore social norms and cross over cultural barriers with the good news of God's forgiveness. They saw him and heard him. That *was* the powerful lesson as he led by example. You can do the same thing with your disciples. Because they are always watching. To be candid, that's the scary part for me; knowing that my wife Deb, knowing that my kids and their mates, my grandkids, and all those at Good News Bible Chapel are watching me. Because like it or not, one way or another, for good or for bad, I am always leading by example, even when I don't say a word.

The last letter, "E" stands for *Encourage*. Jesus never missed an opportunity to encourage his disciples. "When Jesus saw Nathanael approaching, he said of him, 'Here is a true Israelite, in whom there is nothing false'" (John 1:47). Jesus publically praised Nathanael's character in another example of public encouragement. "The woman came and knelt before him. 'Lord, help me!" she said.' he replied, 'It is not right to take the children's bread and toss it to their dogs.' 'Yes, Lord,' she said, 'but even the dogs eat the crumbs that fall from their masters' table.' Then Jesus answered, 'Woman, you have great faith! Your request is granted.' And her daughter was healed from that very hour" (Matthew 15:25). Jesus publically affirmed her faith. Matthew records for us a third example of public encouragement: "'But what about you?' he asked 'Who do you say I am?' Simon Peter answered, 'You are the Christ, the Son of the living God.' Jesus replied, 'Blessed are you, Simon son of Jonah, for this was not revealed to you by man, but by my Father in heaven'" (Matthew 16:15). There were times when Jesus had to publically rebuke and correct Peter who was pretty impulsive with his mouth; a loose cannon. But Jesus also didn't miss the opportunities to publically praise him when he got it right. Affirmation, praise, and public recognition are all part of the best practices of discipling that we can learn from Jesus.

So *who* do you disciple? Well, believe it or not you are already neck deep in discipling relationships. Your wife or husband. Your kids or grandkids. If they are believers, they are your primary discipling ministry. In fact, be clear that it is not the responsibility of the local church or the pastor, the Sunday School teacher or the Youth Ministry Team to disciple your children—that is *your* job.[51] How about your nieces and nephews? The kids in your Sunday School class. The students that you serve in Youth Ministry. The young couple that just got married. The young mom or dad with their first kids. The other people in your Care Group. The person that you led to the Lord last year. All are legitimate discipling opportunities. Opportunities not to be missed.

The key idea, the strategy behind discipling is multiplication. In 2 Timothy 2:2, the apostle Paul coaches his protégée, his disciple, Timothy and says "And the things you have heard me say in the presence of many witnesses entrust to reliable men who will also be qualified to teach others." That's a key verse. Underline that one. Get that progressive sequence of multiplication? I disciple you and a few others. Then you and each of *them* disciple a few others. And each of *them* disciples a few others. The wonder of compound multiplication!

---

[51] You certainly should enlist all the excellent resources of the church to help you get your job done, but don't misunderstand that the primary responsibility for discipling your family is yours, not that of the church. The "professionalism" of our current Western resources like Sunday School and Youth Ministries too easily disguise and usurp the primary responsibility of parents for overseeing their child's spiritual development.

Digging deeper...

● Read 2 Timothy 2:2. Based on what you just read, summarize the key elements of making a disciple.

● Have you ever been discipled/mentored in your faith? By who? What was that like?

● Take a moment now to write down the names of three people that you have some relationships with—people in your circle of influence, people that you can begin to pray for and reach out to disciple. Step one, pray about this opportunity. Step two, identify them. Step three, invite them. Step four, start doing life together!

1.

2.

3.

Pray >   *Identify>*   *Invite >*   *Do life!*

CHAPTER 13

Obeying Jesus

"Whoever has my commands and obeys them, he is the one who loves me. He who loves me will be loved by my Father, and I too will love him and show myself to him."

- John 14:21

Let's refocus on learning to obey the commands of Jesus. Because you can't say that you're faithfully following Jenny Craig if you're not doing what her diet program calls for. That's just wishful thinking. You can't say that you're really a student of Karate if you're not practicing what the Sensei teaches. That's just a poser, a pretender. And you can't claim to be a follower of Jesus if you are not willing to be obedient to what he commanded.

There are at least three reasons why you as an authentic disciple of Jesus must follow his commands. First, obedience to the commands of Jesus helps to confirm your salvation. 1 John 2:3 says "We know that we have come to know him if we obey his commands." There is more to assurance of your salvation than obedience. But this scripture tells us that obedience is a critical part of assurance. If you have no desire to obey the commands of Jesus, then there is good reason to for you to question if you are genuinely born-again by the Spirit of God.

Second, obeying the commands of Jesus is essential to an intimate relationship with Jesus. You can't honestly say that you really want a growing, deeper relationship with Jesus if you are not willing to obey his commands. The intimacy of your relationship is directly connected to your obedience. 1 John 3:24 tells us that "Those who obey his commands live in him, and he in them." John 14:21: "Whoever has my commands and obeys them, he is the one who loves me. He who loves me will be loved by my Father, and I too will love him and show myself to him." That is a powerful promise: Jesus will reveal himself to those who obey him. Could it be that in our obedience, we begin to become more and more like Jesus, his character begins to be formed in us? "...until Christ is formed in you" (Galatians 4:19).

Third, Ethan Tirrell[52] said that obeying the commands of Jesus is the natural response of anyone who says that they love God. 1 John 5:3 says "This is love for God: to obey his commands." In fact, Jesus said that obedience to his command is the sign—it's the test of authentic, genuine love for him. John 14:15: "If you love me, you will obey what I command."

I don't want you to miss the point here. Obedience to the commands of Jesus by a real disciple of Jesus is not optional. Don't go around calling yourself a Christian, a Christ-follower, a lover of Jesus, if you are not willing to obey his commands. Don't put a "Honk if you love Jesus!" bumper sticker on your car, wear a cool Jesus t-shirt, download a neat Christian song for your ring-tone, call yourself a Christian on your Facebook page, wear a cross or a nifty wristband telling everyone that you are a born-again Christian, a follower of Jesus, if you are not willing to do what he commands. The world is full of Christian wanna-bees and fakes, posers and phonies who do who do nothing for the Kingdom of God and in fact hurt the cause of Christ, and, worst of all, deceive themselves into thinking that they are saved. It's better to be quiet and obedient than be loud and disobedient. "Does the LORD delight in burnt offerings and sacrifices as much as in obeying the voice of the LORD? To obey is better than sacrifice, and to heed is better than the fat of rams" (1 Samuel 15:22). It's better to skip the Facebook profile and obey Jesus than use cool Christian images on Facebook and disobey his commands. It's better to save your words and live your love for Jesus out loud. Jesus

---

[52] Ethan Tirrell in a sermon, "Loving God ...," at Good News Bible Chapel, August 8, 2010.

said "Let your light so shine before men, that they may see your good works, and glorify your Father which is in heaven" (Matthew 5:16).

I don't want you to miss the first focus: we need to learn to obey the commands of Jesus. Now, just to be clear, before we go to the second focus I think I need to insert a short, but really important, parenthesis here: *Your obedience is not what saves you.* "For it is by grace you have been saved, through faith—and this not from yourselves, it is the gift of God—not by works, so that no one can boast" (Ephesians 2: 8 & 9). The next verse, verse 10, actually puts our obedience into the proper order: "For we are God's workmanship, created in Christ Jesus to do good works, which God prepared in advance for us to do." You have been chosen by the Father, redeemed by the Son, and sealed by the Spirit (you can see that powerful triple-truth in Ephesians chapter 1) so that then you can do what you were created for: you "are God's workmanship, created in Christ Jesus to do good works, which God prepared in advance for you to do." Faith in the saving death of Jesus on the cross in your place comes first. Obedience to his commands is the only natural and fitting response to that act of love and grace.

Do you remember the three stories in Luke 15 that reveal the heart of God? Here's the setting: "Now the tax collectors and 'sinners' were all gathering around to hear him. But the Pharisees and the teachers of the law muttered, 'This man welcomes sinners and eats with them.'" So the setting here is clear: Jesus is having lunch with the Jewish tax guys who collaborated with the Roman occupiers by collecting taxes from their fellow Jews, plus a hefty service fee for themselves, and passing on the tax money to the Romans. Not too many of us like the IRS; the Publicans or tax collectors of Jesus' day were hated and held in contempt by everyone. So Jesus is having lunch with them and with "sinners," a catch-all term for law breakers, Jews who didn't faithfully try to keep the 613 Mitzvah or commandments. And the law-keepers, the Pharisees and teachers of the law muttered, "This man welcomes sinners and eats with them." Jesus told them three short parables—earthly stories with heavenly meanings—three stories to try to reveal to them the heart of God.

Look at verse 3: "Then Jesus told them this parable: 'Suppose one of you has a hundred sheep and loses one of them. Does he not leave the ninety-nine in the open country and go after the lost sheep until he finds it? And when he finds it, he joyfully puts it on his shoulders and goes home. Then he calls his friends and neighbors together and says, 'Rejoice with me; I have found my lost sheep.' I tell you that in the same way there will be more rejoicing in heaven over one sinner who repents than over ninety-nine righteous persons who do not need to repent.'" What does that story tell you about the heart of God?

Verse 8 continues, "Or suppose a woman has ten silver coins and loses one. Does she not light a lamp, sweep the house and search carefully until she finds it? And when she finds it, she calls her friends and neighbors together and says, 'Rejoice with me; I have found my lost coin.' In the same way, I tell you, there is rejoicing in the presence of the angels of God over one sinner who repents." What does *that* story tell you about the heart of God?

In verse 11 Jesus continued: "There was a man who had two sons. The younger one said to his father, 'Father, give me my share of the estate.' So he divided his property between them." For those Palestinian peasants, politeness and respect to your father was, and still is, paramount. Even if you didn't obey your father, the ancient culture of the community demanded that you had to be polite to him. Rudeness to your father or public disobedience to him was the worst thing you could do; you shamed your father, you shamed your family, and you shamed yourself. This younger son didn't love his father and showed no respect for him. In fact, he acted as if he wished his father was dead. He couldn't wait for his father to die. He wanted his share of the estate now. According to Deuteronomy 21:17, the younger son's share was one third of his father's estate. The father might have had to sell some of his land and his flocks quickly, at cheap prices, to come up with the cash. But he did it.

The parable continues in verse 13: "Not long after that, the younger son got together all he had (he took all of the cash from the sales and everything else that he owned, lock, stock and barrel), and set off for a distant country and there squandered his wealth in wild living." What does that mean, a foreign country? It means that he went outside of Israel and he spent his father's fortune on Gentiles, on a luxurious, extravagant lifestyle with non-believers. That's where we get the common title for this story: the Prodigal Son, because the word prodigal actually means *recklessly extravagant.*

Apparently the young man spent everything that he had: "After he had spent everything, there was a severe famine in that whole country, and he began to be in need. So he went and hired himself out to a citizen of that country, (most likely a Gentile, not a God-fearer, one who didn't respect the Jewish dietary laws) who sent him to his fields to feed pigs. (Maybe that Gentile famer had a good laugh, sending a Jewish boy out to feed the pigs that he'd have for supper.) He longed to fill his stomach with the pods that the pigs were eating, but no one gave him anything."

One of the commentators writes: "So desperate was the young man, that he had to swallow every drop of his pride, national and personal pride, and go do it. And he felt like a pig; he was willing to eat what they ate. *This* is the picture of our desperation at every sin; but we need to feel it if we are to experience the path back to the Father."[53]

Verse 17: "When he came to his senses, he said, 'How many of my father's hired men have food to spare, and here I am starving to death! I will set out and go back to my father and say to him: Father, I have sinned against heaven and against you. I am no longer worthy to be called your son; make me like one of your hired men.' So he got up and went to his father." He was desperate. He rehearsed his apology and headed back home.

But there was a problem. The pride of the name and reputation of your family, of your village, of your inheritance, was so strong, that any act that brought dishonor on your father also brought dishonor on the whole family and the entire village. A first century Jewish ceremony that we find in the *Babylonian Talmud*[54] explains that if a Jewish boy

---

[53] Kenneth E. Bailey, *The Cross and the Prodigal: Luke 15 Through The Eyes Of Middle Eastern Peasants*. (Downers Grove: IVP, 2nd edition, 2005), p. 52.
[54] *Babylonian Talmud: Kethuboth* 28b. See Note 31.

dishonored his family and village by selling a family heirloom to an outsider or losing the family inheritance among the Gentiles and then dared to return home, the community would meet him in the street and surround him, they would throw down and break a large cask of fruit in front of him and cry out "So-in-so is cut off from his people!" This ritual was called the *Ke-za'-zah* (literally "the cutting off") ceremony. After it was performed, the community would have nothing to do with the disobedient and disrespectful person. By selling his inheritance and taking it with him the prodigal son had taken a huge risk; and by losing the inheritance money among the Gentiles, he burned his bridges and had no way to return home. He had no more "rights" to claim and no one would take him in. But listen to how Jesus' story plays out. Verse 20...

"But while he was still a long way off, his father (who must have been watching each day for him to return) saw him and was filled with compassion for him; he *ran* to his son, threw his arms around him and kissed him." In *Prodigal God*,[55] Tim Keller writes "Most of Jesus' listeners would have never seen a Middle Eastern patriarch respond like this. The father patiently endured a tremendous loss of honor and wealth as well as the pain of rejected love. Ordinarily when our love is rejected we get angry, we retaliate, and we do what we can to diminish our affection for the rejecting person, so we won't hurt so much. But this father maintains his affection for his son and bears the agony."

(Listen, a little side conversation here—how do you maintain your affection for someone who has hurt you? How to keep on loving someone you used to love but has become unlovely? You pray for them. Every day you pray for God's blessing on them and the full restoration of your relationship. It is hard to stay angry with someone, it' hard to have an unforgiving attitude, it's hard to lack compassion when you are praying daily for God's mercy and blessing on the one you're separated from. A recent study on spiritual life[56] showed that those couples who

---

[55] Timothy Keller. *The Prodigal God: Recovering The Heart Of The Christian Faith* (New York: Dutton Adult, 2008).
[56] 2006 National Survey on Religion and Family Life. See http://content.usatoday.com/communities/Religion/post/2010/08/happiness-marriage-prayer-bible/1

prayed for each other daily did in fact stay together at much higher rates than those who didn't pray for their mate.)

Back to our story. David J. Miller[57] writes "The father's actions are costly; a senior citizen who gathered up his robes, embarrassing himself yet again by exposing his legs and running down the street like a school child; it was humiliating, shocking. The father is expressing his heart-felt love for his son, but he also has in mind the *kezazah* ceremony." An expert in Jewish culture and customs, Ken Bailey[58] reminds us that the father *had* to reach his son before the villagers; only by a public reconciliation could he keep that shameful cutting-off ceremony from being played out. But to achieve that would require public, self-emptying humiliation on the part of the father. And that's exactly what he does!

(Another side conversation; forgive me… Phil Ryken, former pastor of Tenth Presbyterian Church in Philadelphia and currently President of Wheaton College, offers some wise advice to all of us parents, drawn from the father's lavish welcome: "So many parents do exactly the opposite" he says, "even Christian parents. When their children start going off in the wrong direction they speak to them with scorn and treat them with shame. They tell embarrassing stories about their own kids to others. Instead of humbling *themselves*, they humiliate their children, even to their destruction. But here, Jesus gives fathers and mothers a better model to follow, redefining what it means to be a godly parent." The father takes the initiative to go out and gather his disobedient, disrespectful, unworthy son into the embrace of his self-humiliating love. "His kiss," Ryken continues, "is not so much a *response* to repentance as it is the *cause* of reconciliation. The costly expression of the father's love comes first. The father initiates. It's preemptive reconciliation…")

Verse 21: "The son said to him, 'Father, I have sinned against heaven and against you. I am no longer worthy to be called your son.'" But the

---

[57] David J. Miller, Vicar, *Redeemer Anglican Orthodox Church Mission* "Luke 15:1- 10, The Lost Sheep And The Lost Coin," a sermon for the third Sunday after Trinity, June 21, 2010.
[58] Kenneth E. Bailey. *Jacob And The Prodigal: How Jesus Retold Israel's Story* (Downers Grove: IVP Academic, 2003), 102.

father interrupts his speech. Verse 22: "But the father said to his servants, 'Quick! Bring the best robe and put it on him. Put a ring on his finger and sandals on his feet. Bring the fattened calf and kill it. Let's have a feast and celebrate. For this son of mine was dead and is alive again; he was lost and is found.' So they began to celebrate." What does that tell you about the heart of God? ...

Verse 25: "Meanwhile, the *older* son was in the field. When he came near the house, he heard music and dancing. So he called one of the servants and asked him what was going on. 'Your brother has come,' he replied, 'and your father has killed the fattened calf because he has him back safe and sound.'"

Verse 28: "The older brother became angry and refused to go in. So his father went out and pleaded with him." To refuse a father's invitation to a family celebration was seen as totally unacceptable, rude, and a personal and public rejection of one's father. One would expect that the older brother would usually have played a prominent role in such feasts. But this rude son refuses to attend.

Verse 29: "But he answered his father, 'Look! All these years I've been *slaving* for you and *never disobeyed your orders*. Yet you never gave *me* even a young goat so I could celebrate with my friends. But when this son of yours...' (Did you catch that sarcasm: "*this son of yours...*", not "my brother," No, "this son of yours") who has squandered your property with prostitutes (talk about rubbing dad's face in it...) he comes home, you kill the fattened calf for him!' 'My son,' the father said, 'you are always with me, and everything I have is yours. But we had to celebrate and be glad, because this brother of yours (notice, not "my son") was dead and is alive again; he was lost and is found.'"

So here's the thing: We've been talking for multiple chapters now about Obeying Jesus. We've looked at the last words of Jesus in Matthew chapter 28, verses 19-20: "...Go and make disciples of all nations, baptizing them in the name of the Father and of the Son and of the Holy Spirit, and *teaching them to obey everything I have commanded you.*" And so we have talked about obeying the seven basic commands of Jesus for every disciple, for everyone who claims to be a follower of Jesus: first, repent and believe; second, be baptized; third, remember me; fourth, love God and neighbor; fifth, pray; sixth, give; and seventh, make disciples. A couple of times now I have challenged you with Jesus' own words: "The one who loves me is the one who obeys my commands." The implication is simple and clear: Don't bother claiming to love Jesus if you're not willing to obey him.

But the story we just saw in Luke 15 of the lost son ends with a camera close-up, not focused on the disobedient son, but on the prodigal son's older brother. Did you catch what is happening there? Look again at Luke 15, verse 29: "But he answered his father, 'Look! All these years I've been slaving for you and never disobeyed your orders. Yet you never gave me even a young goat so I could celebrate with my friends!" What's going on here? In *The Prodigal God*,[59] where the father was the prodigal one because of his recklessly extravagant grace and forgiveness, Tim Keller points out that one brother was a law breaker, the other son was a law keeper. But it becomes clear that neither brother loves or respects their father.

While it is pretty obvious that the wastrel son had little love or respect for his father—after all, he's one we quickly identify as a sinner who needs a savior; yet the closing lines of the story make it quite clear that the older son—the obedient one, the one who had done everything right and had always obeyed all that the father had commanded—he had no love and no respect for his father either. (This must have been a rude slap to the law-obeying Pharisees listening to Jesus' three parables.)

It sure seems that the elder son, instead of obeying out of a heart of love for his father, obeyed out of obligation and a very real sense of entitlement, an expectation that he deserved to get something in return for his life-long obedience. And it seems that in his obedience and "goodness" the older son thought he was somehow better than the prodigal when in fact he was just as lost. Keller writes "There are two ways to be your own Savior and Lord. One is by breaking all the moral laws and setting your own course; and one is by keeping all the moral

---

[59] Timothy Keller. *The Prodigal God: Recovering the Heart of the Christian Faith.* (NYC: Dutton, 2008).

laws and being very, very good."⁶⁰ They were both lost sons; one left and one stayed home, but both were equally lost. What both brothers needed was a savior: one knew it, but the other didn't. One slept with the pigs and stank like a pig and knew his desperate need for a savior. One was clean and clueless, blinded by his own obedience into thinking he was close to the father.

Which brother do you think, as the story closes, loves the father more? The rebellious, disrespectful and command-breaking younger son, the one who is forgiven all? Or the very obedient, command-keeping, first-born brother; angry, bitter and resentful, refusing to come to the party? Jesus said, "He who is forgiven much loves much" (Luke 7:47). Sometimes our well-intentioned efforts at being obedient can cloud the picture. Sometimes our apparent goodness can blind us to our desperate need for a savior. And that's the problem with religion. All the world's great religions say you can get and maintain a right relationship with God by obedience to laws and rules and commands. *If you just submit to these rules, obey these commands, follow these paths, practice these disciplines, you'll be okay in the end.* But the Christian faith of the Bible says that you get into and you maintain a relationship with God by God's grace alone. Again, in the words of Philip Yancy, "There is nothing that you can do to make God love you more; and there is nothing that you can do to make God love you less."⁶¹ "For it is by grace you have been saved, through faith—and this not from yourselves, it is the gift of God—not by works, so that no one can boast" (Ephesians 2:8, 9). God already did it all in sending his one and only, perfect son Jesus to the cross to die in your place and mine.

In their insightful book, *True Faced*,⁶² Bruce McNichol, John Lynch and Bill Thrall offer a very thought-provoking chapter called "To please or to trust." Picture a country road entering the woods with a fork in the road up ahead. As you get closer, you see that the sign at the fork

---

⁶⁰ Timothy Keller. *The Prodigal God,* 44.

⁶¹ Philip Yancy, *What's so amazing about grace?* (Grand Rapids: Zondervan, 1997), 70.

⁶² Bill Thrall, Bruce McNichol & John Lynch. *TrueFaced: Trust God And People With Who You Really Are* (Colorado Springs: Nav Press, 2004), 83-106.

pointing to the left says "Pleasing God." The sign pointing to the right says "Trusting God." Which way should you go? Pleasing God sounds good, sounds like the thing that Christ followers should set as a life-goal. After all, the apostle Paul encourages us to "please God in every way" (Colossians 1:10). And anyway, isn't that what obeying Jesus means: pleasing God in every way? But McNichol *et al* write that too often, those traveling down the road called "Pleasing God" find that it leads us to a dead-end at a house with a sign out front that says "The Room of Good Intentions." And inside The Room of Good Intentions are a roomful of sincere, dedicated Christians whose lives are all about pleasing God. But when you listen in on the conversations in that room, you hear story after story of disappointment, discouragement and despair: disappointment from trying hard but not being able to always please God; discouragement from trying hard always to obey perfectly and always falling short; and despair with looking ahead and never seeing a time when you are able to please God in *every* way.

So you leave the Room of Good Intentions and go back down the road to the fork, and take the *other* path, the one marked "Trusting God." And as you travel down *that* road, you discover that that road ends at a house with a sign out front that says "The Room of Grace." And in that room you find sincere, dedicated Christians who recognize their brokenness, admit their inability to obey perfectly, to please God in every way, and, instead of being overwhelmed by disappointment, discouragement, and despair, they *rest—rest* in the Father's deep love shown at the cross; trusting the great love and grace of the Father that was demonstrated at the cross, and they are working together daily with the Father on the rough spots of life. Your choice: pleasing God, or trusting God.

As we wrestle with what it means to authentically obey the commands of Jesus today at school and at work, at home and in the dorm, on the team and in the family, I want to leave you with three closing thoughts. First, don't fool yourself into thinking that you have a relationship with Jesus just because you are obeying his commands. That's the older brother's mistake. And I see it all the time with kids raised in Christian homes, homeschooled kids of Christian parents, students at Christian schools and colleges, adults who have been in the church for years. They mistake *obedience* for relationship. Big mistake. An older brother mistake. Very possibly an eternal fatal error. Examine yourself and your motives carefully. Remember, it's not about rules; it's about a relationship.

So first, don't fool yourself into thinking that you have a relationship with Jesus just because you are obeying his commands.

Second, don't fool yourself into thinking that you love Jesus if you're *not* obeying his commands. To presume on the grace of God is a dangerous thing. Jesus said, "If you love me, you will obey what I command. Whoever has my commands and obeys them, he is the one who loves me" (John 14:15, 21a). I see too many Christians, living in "grace," and "Sinning more so that grace may abound" (Romans 6:1). If you don't have a guilty conscience about your willful disobedience, then maybe you need to do some serious soul searching about your so-called *"love for Jesus."*

Third, if we are going to be authentic, obedient disciples of Jesus then we will "...Go and make disciples of all nations, baptizing them in the name of the Father and of the Son and of the Holy Spirit, and teach them to obey everything Jesus has commanded."

Digging deeper...

● What are the three reasons in the opening paragraphs of this chapter for obeying the commands of Jesus?

● Of the two brothers in the Prodigal Father story — one knew he needed grace, the other seemed to do everything right and didn't know he needed grace too — which brother is most like you? Take time right now to talk with God about that. Write out your thoughts here...

● Which room are you living in: "The Room of Good Intentions?" Or "The Room of Grace?" Where do you want to be? Take some time to pray about this and listen for God's healing assurance from Ephesians 2:8 and 9 *"For by grace you are saved, through faith—and all this is a gift of God—not of works lest anyone should boast."* Write out your prayer to God...

- What has been the most significant message from God to you in this study? Capture that by writing it down here.

- Assignment: What is the next step you need to take in Obeying Jesus? Write it down here ... and your plan to do it!

*"Now that you know these things,
you will be blessed if you do them."*
- Jesus, the Christ, John 13:17

APPENDIX

A list of the commands of Jesus

Many have attempted to compile lists of all the commands of Jesus found in the gospels. A quick Google search of "Commands of Christ" yields more than 8.7 million results and shows that most of these lists agree in general but not in the particulars. While some lists have as few as 38 commands, others suggest more than 100. This difference is explained by observing that some commands are repetitions and others that are "extensions" of a briefer statement. For example, the command to deny yourself is given in Luke 9:23; and is repeated in Matthew 10:38 and again in Mark 8:34. While some are clear statements, "A new commandment I give to you...," others are less direct and might be seen as generic "teaching" rather than an explicit command. Still other commands were directed to an individual, such as the command to Peter to "feed my sheep" (John 21:15-16), yet are taken as commands to all Christ-followers. Most lists find around 50 distinct commands.

Many of the commands for Jesus are repeated or restated elsewhere in the Bible.[63] For example, the command of Jesus to rejoice found in Matthew 5:12 is repeated by the Apostle Paul in 2 Corinthians 6:10 and again 12:10 and also restated by the Apostle James in James 1:2-4. And some of Jesus' commands repeat or echo commands found in the Old Testament such as the command to listen to God's voice found in Matthew 15:11 which echoes that given in 1 Kings 19:11-13.

---

[63] Shown below in parentheses

Here is one such list of the commands of Jesus, compiled and edited by Dave Ahl,[64] which identifies 50 distinct commands.

1. Repent—Matthew 4:17; Luke 13:3
2. Let not your heart be troubled—John 14:27; 16:33; Matthew 6:25-26
3. Follow me—Matthew 4:19
4. Rejoice—Matthew 5:12
5. Let your light shine—Matthew 5:16
6. Honor God's law—Matthew 5:17-19
7. Be reconciled—Matthew 5:24-25
8. Do not commit adultery—Matthew 5:27-30
9. Keep your word—Matthew 5:33-37
10. Go the second mile—Matthew 5:38-42
11. Love your enemies—Matthew 5:44
12. Be perfect—Matthew 5:48
13. Practice secret disciplines (giving, praying, fasting)—Mt 6:1-18
14. Lay up treasures in heaven—Matthew 6:19-21
15. Seek first the kingdom of God—Matthew 6:33
16. Judge not—Matthew 7:1-2
17. Do not throw your pearls to pigs—Matthew 7:6
18. Ask, seek, and knock—Matthew 7:7-8
19. Do unto others—Matthew 7:12
20. Choose the narrow way—Matthew 7:13-14
21. Beware of false prophets—Matthew 7:15
22. Pray for those who spread the word—Matthew 9:37-38
23. Be as shrewd as serpents—Matthew 10:16 (Rom 16:19)
24. Fear God. Do not fear man— Matthew 10:28; Luke 12:4-5
25. Listen to God's voice—Matthew 11:15; 13:9; 13:43; Mark 4:23; Luke 14:35
26. Take my yoke—Matthew 11:29

---

[64] Dave Ahl (www.biblestudymen.com) based his list on the list developed by Bill Gothard. Dave's list can be found on his blog at http://www.swapmeetdave.com/Bible/Commands/Commands-list.pdf

27. Honor your parents—Matthew 15:4
28. Beware of false teaching—Matthew 16:6, 11-12
29. Deny yourself—Luke 9:23; Matthew 10:38; Mark 8:34
30. Do not despise little ones—Matthew 18:10
31. Go to Christians who offend you—Matthew 18:15; (Gal. 6:1)
32. Forgive offenders—Matthew 18:21-22 (Proverbs 19:11)
33. Beware of covetousness—Luke 12:15
34. Honor marriage—Matthew 19:6, 19:9
35. Lead by being a servant—Matthew 20:26-28
36. Make the church a house of prayer for all nations—Mark 11:17
37. Pray in faith—Matthew 21:21-22; John 15:7
38. Bring in the poor—Luke 14:12-14
39. Render unto Caesar—Matthew 22:19-21
40. Love the Lord—Matthew 22:37-38
41. Love your neighbor—Matthew 22:39
42. Be born again—John 3:7
43. Await my return—Matthew 24:42-44
44. Remember Jesus with the Lord's Supper—Matthew 26:26-27
45. Watch and pray—Matthew 26:41
46. Keep my commandments—John 14:15
47. Feed my sheep—John 21:15-16
48. Make and baptize disciples—Matthew 28:19
49. Teach disciples to obey—Matthew 28:20
50. Receive God's power—Luke 24:49

Notes...

About The Author

Steve DuPlessie was adopted by God on September 10, 1957 when he was five years old. The next significant life event was marrying Deb. Three kids quickly followed, now all married to believing spouses and multiplied to seven grandkids.

After working in the marketplace for 25 years in an advertising agency Steve was asked in 2005 to serve as the teaching pastor at Good News Bible Chapel in Attleboro, Massachusetts (USA) where the family has worshipped for decades. His primary ministry is in preaching and making disciples, teaching the body of Christ by example how to get outside the walls of the Chapel and unite with the church of Attleboro to love the city of Attleboro in simple, practical and generous ways. He is a co-founder of *The Saltshaker* in Attleboro, a multi-fellowship, cross-denominational compassion ministry.

Steve and Deb enjoy kayaking the rivers of New England, quiet late night suppers, and getting lots of family time. He was educated at Rhode Island College (BA – Psychology) and Gordon-Conwell Theological Seminary (MA – Urban Ministry).

Also by Steve DuPlessie...

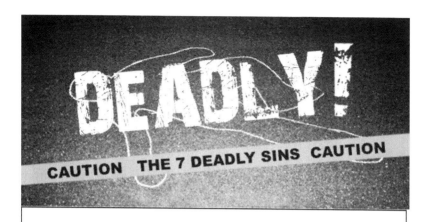

Deadly!
Confronting the seven deadly sins

All the sins on the ancient list called *The Seven Deadly Vices* are still with us today. Some like Lust are amplified by our technology. Some like Greed and even Pride are valued and promoted as character strengths. Envy and Gluttony are the foundation of corporate marketing plans worldwide. The news headlines are filled with tragic reports of Anger. And even Sloth is all around us, not only in the ubiquitous litter that lines our streets and highways, but in smaller, unseen habits (or the lack thereof) of our private lives.

They may be ancient, but they are all still here. And like all sins they are still deadly. And they are still confronted directly—and helpfully—by the teaching of Jesus. In *Deadly!* Steve DuPlessie exposes the old vices and introduces their corresponding virtues for the 21st century.

Available from Anapauo Press and online in paper and E-reader format from amazon.com.

Made in the USA
Charleston, SC
16 September 2012